A Brief Walk through Christian History

A Brief Walk through Christian History

Discover the People, Movements, and Ideas That Transformed Our World

Justin Gatlin

THOM S. RAINER, SERIES EDITOR

TYNDALE
MOMENTUM®

A Tyndale nonfiction imprint

Visit Tyndale online at tyndale.com.

Visit Tyndale Momentum online at tyndalemomentum.com.

Tyndale, Tyndale's quill logo, *Tyndale Momentum*, and the Tyndale Momentum logo are registered trademarks of Tyndale House Ministries. Tyndale Momentum is a nonfiction imprint of Tyndale House Publishers, Carol Stream, Illinois.

A Brief Walk through Christian History: Discover the People, Movements, and Ideas That Transformed Our World

For information about special discounts for bulk purchases, please contact Tyndale House Publishers at csresponse@tyndale.com, or call 1-855-277-9400.

Library of Congress Cataloging-in-Publication Data

A catalog record for this book is available from the Library of Congress.

ISBN 978-1-4964-7368-4

Printed in the United States of America

29	28	27	26	25	24	23
7	6	5	4	3	2	1

Contents

Preface

WHILE THE FIRST CENTURY of our era was still young and the Roman Empire still strong, the brief ministry of Jesus of Nazareth ended with the sealing of his corpse in a cave—crushing his followers' dreams of a conquering Messiah.

Then something incredible happened. According to Jesus' closest followers, he rose from the dead, returned to Jerusalem for a period of weeks to teach them, and then ascended into heaven, leaving them with a message and a mission:

> I have been given all authority in heaven and on earth.
> Therefore, go and make disciples of all the nations,
> baptizing them in the name of the Father and the Son
> and the Holy Spirit. Teach these new disciples to obey all
> the commands I have given you. And be sure of this: I am
> with you always, even to the end of the age.[1]

The resurrection of Jesus turned his bloody murder at Calvary from Rome's seeming triumph into the victory of God over the power of sin and death. The commission he left to his followers would come to define their identity—and that of all subsequent believers as well.

There are many ways to organize a study of Christian history. We could trace the development of doctrines, examine the interaction between believers and the broader society, or recount the biographies of noteworthy men and women whose lives continue to influence our thoughts and actions today. Those are all valid approaches, and I will use them all at points in this book. But I believe the most organic, most helpful way to think about the story of the church is to view it in the context of the instructions Jesus gave before he ascended to heaven.

This is the story of God's children taking light into the darkness—sometimes well, often poorly—declaring that the forces of evil may look powerful in the night, but joy comes with the morning.

With that in mind, each chapter will cover a historical period and reflect on it in three sections. First, we will see how Christians in that era attempted to "go." What were their approaches to evangelism and missions? How did Christianity spread or shift during that period? Second, reflecting on the commandment to baptize, we will examine how the boundaries of the faith were set during that period. What defined a Christian? Who was "in" or "out"? How did church governance reflect those ideas? Finally, we will look at doctrine and practice during each era, as followers of Jesus were taught to obey what he had commanded. What doctrines were clarified or disputed? What did worship look like?

Apart from the chapters on the Empire period (beginning with the conversion of Constantine) and the Reformation—which are understandably longer—the other chapters are roughly the same length. The one exception is the chapter on the twentieth century, in which I cover events that may eventually prove to be blips on the historical radar, but are still important for those of us living in their aftermath.

My prayer is that this structure will make the applicability of history to modern life as clear as possible. We have the same responsibility and face similar challenges as those who have gone before us. May we continue to make disciples, knowing that Jesus is with us still—even to the end of the age.

1

The Setting
of Christian History

(333 BC–AD 30)

MANY BOOKS ON THE SETTING of the New Testament reference
Galatians 4:4: "When the right time came, God sent his Son, born
of a woman, subject to the law."[1] Whether the early Christians
realized it or not, God had prepared the world for the rapid explosion of the gospel. The common use of the Greek language, the
philosophical milieu of the Roman era, the relative stability of the
Pax Romana, and the Jewish diaspora all created an environment
ripe for transformation.

The Hellenistic Period (333–320 BC)

In late 2011, three separate wildfires in Central Texas merged
into one gigantic conflagration. The resulting blaze killed four
people and caused hundreds of millions of dollars in damage.[2]
Firefighters worked bravely for more than a month to bring the

fires under control and another four weeks to extinguish them completely. Even today, more than a decade later, visitors to the Lost Pines Forest can see obvious marks of the devastation. The fire spread rapidly and uncontrollably for a short amount of time, stopped suddenly, and permanently transformed everything it touched. I can think of no better metaphor for the career of Alexander III of Macedon (356–323 BC), commonly known as Alexander the Great.

Many ancient kings were called "the Great" by their admirers, but Alexander is one who earned the title. Though he died suddenly of a fever at the age of thirty-two, during his brief lifetime he conquered Greece and pushed his empire as far as modern-day Pakistan. The empire did not last long without him, but the aftereffects far outlived his reign. It is impossible to understand the history of the Mediterranean without recognizing the transformation of the language, culture, and politics of the region under Alexander.

Though the Greek language and culture had already spread east before the time of Alexander, his rule accelerated and intensified this movement. Having been tutored personally by Aristotle, Alexander was saturated in Greek culture, but his primary goal was conquest; spreading the culture was a means, not an end. As regions were conquered, their gods were assimilated with the Greek gods and their ideas adopted into the broader philosophy. This amalgamation is known as *Hellenism*. The cultural changes ranged across the spectrum, leading to the adoption of Greek thought, dress, and culture to varying degrees in different geographic areas and levels of society. For the Jews in Palestine, and later the Christians across southern Europe and Asia Minor, religious syncretism was unacceptable. They worshiped one God, and he could not be identified with Zeus any more than he had been with Ra in Egypt.[3]

The Ptolemaic (320–198 BC) and Seleucid (198–167 BC) Periods

When Alexander died, his empire was divided between several of his top generals. One of these was Ptolemy (pronounced with a silent *P*), who took control of Egypt, setting up his capital in Alexandria. He also deposed the governor of Palestine in 320 BC. Josephus (an important Jewish historian who lived from AD 37–100) describes the conquest:

> [Ptolemy] seized Jerusalem by resorting to cunning and deceit. For he entered the city on the Sabbath as if to sacrifice, and, as the Jews did not oppose him—for they did not suspect any hostile act—and, because of their lack of suspicion and the nature of the day, were enjoying idleness and ease, he became master of the city without difficulty and ruled it harshly.[4]

After the initial invasion, Ptolemy seems to have softened his approach.

This cultural transformation was sufficiently successful that during the reign of his son, Ptolemy II Philadelphus, the Old Testament was translated for a Jewish culture now more comfortable with Greek than with their ancestral Hebrew. The Septuagint (abbreviated LXX) is an uneven translation, but it was often—though not exclusively—quoted by the New Testament authors and early church fathers. As the original preface to the King James Version puts it, "The translation of the Seventy [Interpreters] dissenteth from the Original in many places, neither doth it come near it, for perspicuity, gravity, majesty; yet which of the Apostles did condemn it? Condemn it? Nay, they used it."[5]

Ptolemy's dynasty continued to reign until Egypt fell to Rome with the death of Cleopatra in 30 BC, but their control over Palestine had ended in 198 BC when Antiochus III of Syria defeated Ptolemy V. Not all Israelites were pleased with the change. The high priest (Onias III) supported the Egyptians, while the wealthy Tobiads supported Syria. At first, the Oniads were able to maintain their power, but Antiochus IV (the self-proclaimed Epiphanes, who said he was the manifestation of Zeus) was much more aggressive and egotistical. He set up Onias's brother, Jason, as a puppet high priest who would funnel the riches of the Temple to Antiochus.

The Maccabean/Hasmonean Period (167–63 BC)

In 167 BC, Antiochus determined to bring the Jewish people into submission by sending an emissary to a village about ten miles north of Jerusalem to enforce sacrifices to the Roman gods. An elderly priest named Mattathias resisted both bribes and threats, personally killed a Jew who attempted to comply, killed the king's emissary, and tore down the altar (1 Maccabees 2:17-26). When he fled with his five sons, a group of the faithful (called Hasideans or "pious ones") came to him and revolted against the Syrians.

Mattathias did not live long enough to see the full fruit of his faithfulness, but his son Judas—nicknamed Maccabeus, or "the Hammer"—was a skilled military commander. Under his leadership, the Maccabees successfully obtained religious freedom in 164 BC, and Judas was able to rededicate the Temple (an achievement still celebrated today at Hanukkah).

Unfortunately, pure motives sometimes go sour. After Judas was killed in battle while still striving for Israelite independence, his brothers proved to be more pragmatic than pious. Jonathan was an effective commander but accepted an appointment as high priest as part of the political machinations of Antiochus's successors. After Jonathan's death, Simon was able to secure Jewish independence in 142 BC, and he also accepted the office of hereditary high priest. Operating as both priest and king, Simon consolidated power just as King Saul had centuries before.

Simon's descendants, called the Hasmoneans, drifted further and further from their Hasidean roots, becoming increasingly Hellenized. The Hasideans eventually evolved into the group we know as the Pharisees, and the wealthy and powerful priestly families evolved into the Sadducees. For Christians, the most famous Hasmoneans were the people of the Herodian dynasty, whose wickedness and corruption were illustrative of the group.

The Roman Period (63 BC–AD 30)

From 264–146 BC, Rome was occupied by Carthage, her chief rival in the Punic Wars. Though initially Carthage had naval superiority, the Romans proved incredibly adaptive in duplicating the enemy's techniques and were ultimately triumphant.[6] This adaptability marked Rome's overall approach, whether it was adopting local deities into their pantheon or leaving local governments in place under Roman domination. Rome's initial forays into Asia Minor were designed to bring peace and stability to a region still fractured by Alexander's successors, but power once taken is rarely surrendered.

After the Maccabean revolt, Israel enjoyed freedom for the first time in centuries. But by 63 BC, the Romans were no longer distracted by other conflicts, and their general Pompey conquered Palestine. The Romans allowed peaceful provinces to exercise local rule within their "law of the province," and each region maintained its distinctive character.[7] Rebellious Palestine was accorded fewer privileges.

Gradually, Julius Caesar coalesced power around himself and became emperor in all but name. Following the assassination of

Julius and the Liberators' Civil War, his nephew Octavian became the first formal emperor of Rome in 27 BC. Octavian took the name Augustus, "the majestic one," declared that Julius was a god, and identified himself as the son of god.

After subduing his internal rivals, and with no important external enemies left, Augustus was the first leader to enjoy the *Pax Romana* (the peace of Rome), which would endure for about two centuries. In AD 14, Augustus's son Tiberius took the throne and reigned during the time of Jesus' earthly ministry. These pieces set the scene for the story of the Christian movement. Wicked rulers at every level, a widespread regional empire, a virtually universal language, and a remarkable peace all prepared the way for the message of Jesus to turn everything upside down.

Evangelism and Expansion

The spread of the Greek language and Hellenistic culture defined the era, creating a common intellectual milieu and facilitating international communication. Greek was the language of both the academy and the marketplace, and the translation of the Old Testament into Greek made the Hebrew Scriptures accessible to outsiders, preparing a newly interconnected world for the preaching of the apostles. A common language was as important in the first century as Gutenberg's printing press was in the fifteenth or the internet is in the twenty-first.

The Old Testament had what is often called a centripetal approach to bringing people to God.[8] Instead of Israel going out to the nations, the nations were expected to be drawn to the glory and blessings of God's chosen people. Gentiles who committed themselves to the Law were circumcised, were given a ritual bath, and performed certain sacrifices were called proselytes (Acts 2:10-11, ESV).

Boundaries of the Community

In the eyes of the governing authorities, there were Romans and there were barbarians. Yet even within Roman society there were several important layers. At the bottom were the slaves, comprising maybe 20 to 40 percent of the population of Rome.[9] Above them were the freemen, former slaves who had obtained emancipation. At the top were full citizens, who themselves fell into two classes, only the highest of whom had the right to vote or hold office. These strata created significant boundaries between classes of people, which could only be overcome by extraordinary circumstances, such as wealth (see Acts 22:28, for example) or patronage from the emperor.

In Israel, the basic distinction was between Jew and Gentile. The rabbis forbade a Gentile woman from nursing a Hebrew child, and it was also forbidden to teach a Gentile boy a craft that would give him a livelihood.[10] During the Ptolemaic period, the rulers took Jews and Samaritans to Egypt and trained them in Hellenistic culture. To a lesser extent, those remaining in Palestine were Hellenized by trade and by the Greek cities in their midst. In backlash to this, other Jews (particularly in the area near Jerusalem) doubled down on their commitment to traditional Hebrew culture.

Discipleship

For the Greeks and their successors, people were discipled primarily through trade and economic might. Jewish boys who wanted the honor of participating in Greek athletic competitions would undergo painful procedures to hide their circumcision, and those who wanted wealth and influence conformed to Roman culture. Within Israel, one of the important developments during this period was the creation of the synagogue. Although the specifics are open to debate, synagogues were an important part of community life that gradually emerged around 300 BC. There the Torah could be read, people could be taught, and disputes could be settled.[11] At the same time, the oral law took on a central place in the lives of the Pharisees, passed on from the rabbi to their students.

2

The Apostolic Period

(AD 30–AD 69)

UNDER THE OPPRESSIVE WEIGHT of Roman taxation, a Galilean Jew named Judas gathered a group of followers and challenged them to reject sinful human authority and fight against the Romans. He and his followers revolted and ultimately paid with their lives.[1] Under the weight of Roman rule and the wicked Hasmoneans, there were many men who tried to follow in the footsteps of the Maccabees and break the chains of Israel's oppressors. Josephus (a renowned Jewish historian) lists several, both before and after the ministry of Jesus. Unfortunately, they ended up with bloodshed, not freedom, until in 70 AD Jerusalem itself was destroyed.

But Jesus was a different kind of leader. "My Kingdom is not an earthly kingdom," he told Pontius Pilate. "If it were, my followers would fight to keep me from being handed over to the Jewish leaders. But my Kingdom is not of this world."[2] While various rebels took up arms, the followers of Jesus announced that he had already conquered the greatest enemy of all: death itself. They traveled throughout the known world, preaching the good news (gospel) that Jesus is Lord. While Judaism had a centripetal mission (pulling the Gentiles into the glory of God's people), Jesus gave his people a centrifugal mission in Acts 1:8: "You will be my witnesses, telling people about me everywhere— in Jerusalem, throughout Judea, in Samaria, and to the ends of the earth." This chapter is the story of how that first generation went out into the world.

Jesus and the Crucifixion

Crucifixion was such a barbarous method of humiliation and execution that the Roman statesman Cicero said it should not even be mentioned in polite society. The Septuagint translation of Deuteronomy 21:23 says that "everyone who is hung on a tree is cursed in the sight of God."[3] Josephus describes the brutality of it:

> I saw many captives crucified; and remembered three of
> them as my former acquaintance. I was very sorry at this
> in my mind, and went with tears in my eyes to Titus, and
> told him of them; so he immediately commanded them
> to be taken down, and to have the greatest care taken of
> them, in order to their recovery; yet two of them died
> under the physician's hands, while the third recovered.[4]

It is no wonder, then, that when Jesus was taken away to be crucified "all his disciples deserted him and ran away" (Mark 14:50). Jesus had called out twelve apostles, in a clear reference to the twelve tribes of Israel, to be the nucleus of his church. One of them, Judas Iscariot, betrayed him and committed suicide.

Another, John the beloved disciple, initially abandoned Jesus but then came to the foot of the cross where he was given responsibility for Jesus' mother, Mary. After Jesus was crucified, stabbed with a spear, and laid in a borrowed tomb, none of the disciples were expecting their victorious king to emerge on the third day. But Christ conquered death and showed himself to his disciples. They were not to merely preach some ideas they believed; they were to be witnesses of what they had seen (1 Corinthians 15:1-9). After spending an additional forty days with the disciples after the Resurrection, Jesus ascended to heaven (Acts 1:9-11) to take his place at the right hand of the Father (Psalm 110:1). Then, at the feast of Pentecost, Jesus sent the Holy Spirit to empower the gathered believers (the *ekklesia*). The once fearful disciples who had run away were now commissioned and prepared to run out and carry the good news of Christ's triumph to the world.

Early Conflicts

Initially, persecution came primarily from the Jewish leaders who had opposed Jesus during his ministry. They now tried to forbid the apostles from preaching about him. Acts 4:20 represents the attitude of Jesus' disciples: "We cannot stop telling about everything we have seen and heard."

When these external attacks were not successful, the enemy took a different approach—fomenting division within the church. In one instance, the Hellenistic believers felt that their widows were being neglected in the daily distribution of food. To resolve this conflict and provide for the physical needs of the church, the congregation selected seven men who were approved by the apostles. The division of labor between the apostles as spiritual leaders, committed to prayer and the ministry of the Word (Acts 6:4), and the seven focusing on the unity of the church and on physical needs establishes the pattern of elders and deacons in later churches (1 Timothy 3).

After this internal crisis was resolved, the external threats crossed a new threshold when one of the seven, Stephen, became the first Christian martyr. The Greek word *martys* refers to "a witness," and thus the English word *martyr* refers to those believers who witnessed for the Lord by sacrificing their lives. Many have followed in Stephen's steps since, but it is hard to think of any who have had a greater impact through their final testimony than he did. One of the people who heard Stephen's message and watched as he died was a young man named Saul of Tarsus (Acts 7:58).

The Conversion of Saul

What began with Stephen did not end with him. Acts 8:3 describes a wave of persecution that swept over the nascent church: "Saul was going everywhere to destroy the church. He went from house to house, dragging out both men and women to throw them into prison." But what the opponents of Christ's followers meant for evil, God meant for good, in at least two ways.

First, the disciples had been instructed by Jesus to take the Good News to the ends of the earth once they received the Holy Spirit, yet at the time of Stephen's death they were still huddled in Jerusalem. This persecution scattered the believers across the Near East and beyond, and they carried the Good News of Christ with them.

Second, Saul's resistance to the gospel did not last forever. As he was traveling to Damascus to persecute the believers there, a dazzling light blinded him and a voice from heaven challenged him. Saul had resisted the Spirit's conviction, but now it was time to respond. He was baptized and became the church's most memorable advocate. Saul went to the synagogues in Damascus and began preaching, and then went into Arabia where he was tutored by the Holy Spirit before returning to Damascus (Galatians 1:17).[5] The believers in Jerusalem were understandably skeptical of Saul's conversion. What kind of trick was this? But Barnabas advocated on Saul's behalf and won his acceptance with the church leaders in Jerusalem. Barnabas turned out to be one of the most consequential figures of all time. Humanly speaking, he was responsible for launching the ministry of the apostle Paul, whose thirteen letters make up the bulk of the New Testament epistles. Without Paul, we would probably not have the Gospel of Luke or the book of Acts. Moreover, when Paul rejected John Mark (who later wrote the Gospel of Mark), Barnabas traveled with him instead, helping the younger man grow and mature. So, in one way or another, the majority of the New Testament can be traced to Barnabas, whose legacy was forged in the impact he had on the lives of others.

The Gospel for the Gentiles

At roughly the same time that Barnabas was getting to know Saul, another important development was taking place in the city of Caesarea. A Roman centurion named Cornelius had a vision of an angel, who instructed him to summon the apostle Peter. Meanwhile, Peter had a vision in which he was instructed not to condemn as unclean what God had cleansed. When Peter arrived, he shared the gospel message with Cornelius, who believed and was baptized.

When Peter reported in Jerusalem what had happened in Caesarea, objections to receiving Gentiles into the church were quickly silenced (Acts 11) and a booming intercultural movement began. At Antioch the believers were first called Christians— that is, partisans of Christ.[6] Barnabas, in a remarkable display of humility, decided he wasn't equal to the task of teaching all the new converts in Antioch, so he went to Tarsus to recruit Saul to help him lead the church and reach the city. They preached together for a year, seeing tremendous success even as James was added to the number of martyrs (Acts 12:2).

Although they're not explicitly mentioned in the biblical account, some important events occurred in the background as the church was finding its feet in the world. The Roman authorities did not distinguish between Jews (who were afforded special protections) and the church that claimed a Jewish Messiah but welcomed Gentiles as well. But as the conflict heated up and the division over Christ became more pronounced, the Roman authorities began to take notice. Suetonius, the Roman historian, observes how Emperor Claudius reacted in AD 41: "Since the Jews constantly made disturbances at the instigation of Chrestus [probably a misspelling of Christ], he expelled them from Rome."[7] This caused some conflict that hovers in the background of Paul's letter to the Romans, where Jewish believers who had been expelled returned and the church struggled to navigate the cultural tensions. More positively, Aquila and Priscilla moved from Rome to Corinth (Acts 18:2) and met Paul there, ultimately becoming influential missionaries.

Paul's Missionary Journeys

A common misconception is that God changed Saul's name to Paul at his conversion—just as he had changed Abram's name to Abraham after making the covenant with him. But Saul continued to go by the Jewish form of his name for several years after his Damascus road experience.

In Acts 13:4, we're told that "Barnabas and Saul were sent out by the Holy Spirit" from Antioch to carry the gospel to new regions. It was on this trip through the cities of South Galatia that Saul stepped fully into his role as apostle to the Gentiles, and from Acts 13:14 on, "Barnabas and Saul" is replaced by "Paul and Barnabas" whenever the two men are mentioned together. Paul was not one of the twelve disciples who walked with Jesus in person, but through a vision of Christ he was commissioned as an apostle (1 Corinthians 15:8-11).

Tradition describes this "born at the wrong time" apostle as bald-headed, with a hooked nose, a long curly beard, and bowed legs.[8] Regardless of whether this description is accurate, Paul by his own admission was neither a physically impressive man nor a great orator (2 Corinthians 10:10). However, his spiritual power and commitment to the gospel whatever it cost him were certainly impressive. After returning to Antioch from his first missionary journey (probably in AD 47–48), he and Barnabas were sent as delegates to the Council of Jerusalem, where the status of Gentiles as full equals in the family of God was established (Acts 15).

Paul's second missionary journey (ca. AD 49–51) included visits to the regions of Anatolia, Macedonia, and Achaia. He probably wrote 1 and 2 Thessalonians during this trip. Initially, Paul and Barnabas were set to travel together, but Barnabas wanted to take along his cousin John Mark, who had abandoned them during their first missionary journey. The issue divided Barnabas and Paul, and they went their separate ways—Barnabas and John Mark to Cyprus, and Paul with a new traveling companion, Silas, to Syria and Cilicia (Acts 15:36-41). What might have been only a story of conflict and division in the early church eventually resulted in reconciliation. Both missionary teams accomplished great things for the Kingdom of God, and Mark went on to have a tremendous impact through his writing of one of the four Gospels in the New Testament. One commentator noted that when the Holy Spirit inspired the Gospel that most clearly portrays Jesus as the perfect, unfailing servant, he chose John Mark, the failed servant, as his instrument.[9] Near the end of Paul's life, he requested that Mark be brought to him in Rome, saying, "He will be helpful to me in my ministry" (2 Timothy 4:11).

Paul's third missionary journey (ca. AD 51–54) took him to Ephesus and various other churches, collecting funds for famine relief in Jerusalem. Even at this early date, we see local churches cooperating with one another to both spread the gospel and meet physical needs. Paul wrote three of his most influential letters, 1 Corinthians, 2 Corinthians, and Romans, during this time.

In AD 55, Paul was arrested on the false charge of bringing Gentiles into the Temple (perhaps a deliberate misunderstanding of his teaching about the unity of the church). Eventually, he exercised his right as a Roman citizen and appealed to the Caesar, Nero, who was no friend of Christians. In fact, Nero allegedly started the Great Fire of Rome in AD 64 to justify rebuilding it to his standards, and then executed Christians as scapegoats. Paul wasn't sentenced during this wave of persecution, but remained under guard for years. While still imprisoned, around AD 58–60, he wrote the so-called prison epistles: Ephesians, Philippians, Colossians, and Philemon. Exact details are hard to come by after this point, but tradition suggests that Paul was released for a time, during which he wrote 1 Timothy and Titus, then was imprisoned again, wrote 2 Timothy from jail, and was executed by decapitation in AD 67.

Paul's legacy is unparalleled. He was the first to bring the gospel to many regions, trained many important leaders, and wrote thirteen letters that became part of the New Testament (and he is sometimes also credited with writing Hebrews). One of his traveling companions, Luke, wrote both the Gospel of Luke and the book of Acts. Other than Jesus himself, no one has had a greater impact on Christianity than the apostle Paul.

The apostle Peter probably was killed about the same time as Paul. According to Eusebius, Peter was crucified upside down in Rome.[10] There is a tradition that Peter started the church at Rome, but this seems unlikely since he is unmentioned in Paul's letter to the Romans. With the death of these two pillars of early Christianity, men who exemplified the mission to the Jews and the Gentiles more clearly than anyone else, the biblical era ended. Though a few of the apostles were likely still alive until the mid-70s and John probably lived past AD 90, the historical account in Acts ends with Paul awaiting trial, and his letters end as he is awaiting execution.

Evangelism and Expansion

Initially, the disciples were so eager to go out into the world that Jesus had to instruct them to wait for the coming of the Holy Spirit. But once the Holy Spirit came, they lingered in Jerusalem until persecution drove them out. This is a recurring theme: Persecution intended to harm the church instead sends people out like spores from a flower driven into the wind. Tertullian wisely observed that the blood of the martyrs was the seed of the church. Whether it was the persecution in Jerusalem, Saul's attempts to drive the church out of existence, or Claudius's decree expelling the Jews from Rome, the enemy's attempts to harm Christ's body served to accelerate the Great Commission.

Boundaries of the Community

During the first generation after the ascension of Christ, the greatest challenge to the church was understanding her relationship to Israel. Did Gentiles need to become circumcised and submit to the law in order to follow the Messiah? Peter's vision before the conversion of Cornelius and the Council at Jerusalem answered this question with a resounding *no*. Galatians, Ephesians, and Hebrews show that there were not different classes of believers. Instead, the boundaries of the community were established by faith in Christ, publicly revealed by baptism. Ethnic distinctions neither separated people from God nor joined them to him. Socioeconomic distinctions were irrelevant: The apostles preached both to beggars and to kings. Faithfulness marked the boundaries: Those who taught falsely about Jesus or those who caused division within the community revealed themselves to be outside the community. While this simplicity didn't last, it is amazing to see how God revealed his power in response to unity in the church, and how threats to unity were seriously resisted.

Discipleship

Because evidence is limited for the processes of discipleship during this era, it can be tempting to read an uncanny resemblance to our own preferences into the text. But we can draw some broad conclusions. In 2 Timothy 2:2, Paul writes, "You have heard me teach things that have been confirmed by many reliable witnesses. Now teach these truths to other trustworthy people who will be able to pass them on to others." This basic pattern is revealed in Acts and in the Epistles. Paul taught Silas, Barnabas taught Mark, and so on. Older women were admonished to teach younger women, and older men to teach younger men. Discipleship during this time wasn't marked by formal schools, but by something similar to the rabbinic model of personal mentorship. The primary responsibility of the elders was the ministry of the Word, and their teaching and preaching challenged people to grow in their faith.

3

The Post-Apostolic Period

(AD 70–AD 120)

In the waning days of Jesus' earthly ministry, his disciples were admiring the buildings of the Temple complex. It isn't difficult to see why. The courtyard walls enclosed about thirty-five acres, the porticoes were fifty feet wide, and the Temple itself was made of dazzling white marble with a gold veneer on the entrance. Beyond its physical beauty and awe-inspiring scale, the Temple was the heart of Israelite worship. But Jesus made an ominous prediction: "Do you see all these buildings? I tell you the truth, they will be completely demolished. Not one stone will be left on top of another!" (Matthew 24:2).

The disciples thought that such destruction must mean the end of the world (Matthew 24:3). And they were almost right: The world as they knew it ended when Titus, the general who would later become emperor, destroyed the city of Jerusalem. Though some of the apostles probably lived past that time—and John certainly did—there were dramatic changes in the world that make it reasonable to refer to AD 70 as the beginning of the post-apostolic period.

The Fall of Jerusalem

Florus, the procurator of Judah in AD 66, was a particularly cruel ruler. The people were used to this kind of treatment, but Josephus (an eyewitness) describes the breaking point: "As to the citizens of Jerusalem, although they took this matter very ill, yet did they restrain their passion; but Florus acted herein as if he had been hired, and blew up the war into a flame, and sent some to take seventeen talents [1,132 pounds] out of the sacred treasure, and pretended that Caesar wanted them."[1] When this was not resolved, the revolutionaries in Jerusalem attacked the Roman garrison. The governor of Syria, Cestius Gallus, was unable to regain control, and Nero sent Vespasian with an army of 60,000 troops to crush the rebellion.

However, Nero's problems were not confined to Palestine. Infighting meant the kingdom (and the first imperial dynasty that had begun with Augustus) began to crumble. When Nero committed suicide with no clear successor, a series of coups occurred in rapid succession. AD 69 is known as the Year of the Four Emperors: Servius Sulpicius Galba, Marcus Salvius Otho, and Aulus Vitellius each reigned briefly until Titus Flavius Vespasianus (known as Vespasian) consolidated power. Vespasian entrusted Palestine to his son Titus and returned to Rome where he was an effective ruler who restored Rome's financial and social stability.

Titus extinguished the Jewish rebellion with brutal efficiency, ultimately burning the Temple. Josephus claims that the destruction of the Temple was accidental, but it is hard to believe that

Titus would have left the center of the revolutionary ideology untouched. This Temple with no idol in the middle was the marker of everything that kept Israel from assimilating, and it was the appropriation of Temple funds that had launched the rebellion in the first place.

Though the revolt lasted a few more years (the last stronghold, Masada, didn't fall until 73), and there were other rebellions until about 135, Israel was forever changed by the defeat. Without the Temple, the nation faced a theological crisis. Before the Exile, the people had engaged in open idolatry; why would God allow them to be overcome again? Without the Temple and its sacrifices, how could they obey the Mosaic law? The Pharisees became dominant in the power struggle that followed. The Zealots and Essenes were apparently destroyed in the war, and the Sadducees were irrelevant without the Temple and political power. Even the Pharisees shifted to some degree, transforming their religion into the rabbinic Judaism that continues in some form to this day.

The First Apostolic Fathers

The church fathers who lived within a generation of the apostles (ca. 70–120) are traditionally called the apostolic fathers. The most important document from this era is the Teaching of the Twelve Apostles (commonly known as the Didache). Some scholars date it as early as AD 70, but it was probably finalized between 90 and 100. Its dependence on Matthew, and particularly the Sermon on the Mount, is obvious from the first chapter:

> Two ways there are, one of life and one of death, but
> there is a great difference between the two ways [Matthew
> 7:13-14]. The way of life, then, is this: First, thou shalt
> love the God who made thee; secondly, thy neighbor as

thyself [Matthew 22:37-39]; and all things whatsoever thou wouldst not have befall thee, thou, too, do not to another [Matthew 7:12]. Now of these words the teaching is this: Bless them that curse you, and pray for your enemies, and fast for them that persecute you: for what thank *have ye* if ye love them that love you? Do not the nations also the same? But love ye them that hate you and ye shall have no enemy [Matthew 5:43-47]. Abstain from the fleshly and worldly lusts. If any one give thee a blow on the right cheek, turn to him the other also, and thou shalt be perfect; if any one compel thee to go one mile, go with him two; if any one take thy cloak, give him thy tunic also; if any one take from thee what is thine, ask it not back; for indeed thou canst not. To every one that asketh thee give, and ask not back; for to all the Father desireth to have given of his own gracious gifts [Matthew 5:38-42]. Blessed is he that giveth according to the commandment; for he is guiltless; woe to him that receiveth; for if, indeed, one receiveth who hath need, he shall be guiltless; but he who hath no need shall give account, why he took, and for what purpose, and coming under confinement shall be examined concerning what he did, and shall not go out thence until he pay the last farthing [Matthew 5:26]. But it hath been also said concerning this *matter*: Let thine alms sweat in thy hands, until thou knowest to whom thou shouldst give.[2]

The Didache includes three parts: an ethical section, a section on church life, and an eschatological conclusion. It was rediscovered in 1873 and provides an important window into the lives of Christians in the period immediately following the completion of the New Testament. Though never included in any Bibles, as far as we know, apparently it was widely used and highly respected.

The book of First Clement holds a different place and was at least occasionally included with the books of the New Testament (see the discussion of the canon in chapter 6, "The Empire Period"). Clement of Rome served as an early bishop of the church at Rome (third, according to Irenaeus), and though the letter is written as if from the whole Roman church (with frequent use of "we"), Clement is traditionally seen as the author. Likely written sometime in the 90s, the letter deals with factions in the congregation and calls them to unity. Clement cites 1 Corinthians explicitly (see 1 Clement 47:1-4) and possibly some other books, though it isn't clear that he viewed them as Scripture. Second Clement was not written by Clement of Rome; most likely, it was penned about fifty years later. It is noteworthy as the earliest surviving post-biblical sermon.

Other important documents are the seven letters of Ignatius (also included in some lists of canonical books), which he wrote on his way to Rome to be executed. Ignatius was the third bishop of the church at Antioch in Syria, which is well known in the book of Acts for sending out Paul and Barnabas. The letters of Ignatius are interesting for many reasons, but they are especially important because they clearly draw from the Gospel of Matthew, Paul's epistles, Hebrews, and 1 John. This shows that the books of the New Testament were circulated as authoritative very soon after they were written, because Ignatius was killed around AD 108, according to Eusebius. This undermines a common objection that the original writings of the apostles were lost or corrupted; to the contrary, the New Testament manuscript evidence and external references such as Clement and Ignatius give us confidence that God has preserved his Word.

Ignatius gives some insight into the structure of the church in his day. Each bishop led one church (not yet a region in the way that episcopal government would develop later). He was apparently supported by elders (or presbyters) and deacons, although in 1 Clement 44 bishops and presbyters are interchangeable, so it's possible the bishop was "first among equals," rather than a distinct office. Ignatius was the first to use the word *catholic* to describe all believers as one universal church, though the term did not become definitive until the fourth century.[3]

Persecution

Rome was generally happy to move forward like a gathering snowball, absorbing pieces of everything in its path. The gods of conquered regions were assimilated as different names for the gods the Romans already worshiped or simply added to the Roman pantheon. As long as the people were willing to swear by the emperor, they were allowed to continue worshiping their gods. A special exemption was granted to the Jews, who had demonstrated with their blood their unwillingness to compromise. And because at first Christianity was considered a branch of Judaism, the early church benefited from the same favorable treatment. But as Christianity and Judaism diverged, the Christians lost their exempt status. Already under Nero, Christians were persecuted not for some specific behavior or crime, but for their adherence to "the name." Here's how Pliny the Younger later described their "crimes" in a letter to Emperor Trajan:

> They had met regularly before dawn on a fixed day to
> chant verses alternately among themselves in honor of
> Christ as if to a god, and also to bind themselves by oath,
> not for any criminal purpose, but to abstain from theft,

robbery, and adultery, to commit no breach of trust and
not to deny a deposit when called upon to restore it. After
this ceremony it had been their custom to disperse and
reassemble later to take food of an ordinary, harmless
kind but they had in fact given up this practice since
my edict, issued on your instructions, which banned all
political societies. This made me decide it was all the more
necessary to extract the truth by torture from two slave-
women, who they call deaconesses. I found nothing but a
degenerate sort of cult carried to extravagant lengths.[4]

What a charge! They claimed the name of Christ, met together
for prayer, promised to live faithfully, took the Lord's Supper, and
shared the *agape* feast, though they had stopped this when Trajan
banned political societies (*collegia*). This kind of language was
rooted in the ways the Romans had treated other dissident groups,
but it is uniquely fitting for the followers of those who, in Acts
5:41, "left the high council rejoicing that God had counted them
worthy to suffer disgrace for the name of Jesus."[5]

Trajan, who reigned from 98 to 117, struck an interesting balance. Merely claiming the name of Christ was a capital offense, but
Christians were not to be actively pursued. He wrote:

These people must not be hunted out; if they are brought
before you and the charge against them is proved, they
must be punished, but in the case of anyone who denies
that he is a Christian, and makes it clear that he is not
by offering prayers to our gods, he is to be pardoned as a
result of his repentance however suspect his past conduct
may be.[6]

The result was that persecution of Christians was inconsistent. In some places, Christians might go for long periods of time without fear. Elsewhere, believers were regularly accused and forced to choose between compromise and death. This tension provided some benefits. Christians were never able to take worldly security for granted, but they had enough stability to continue developing their theology and growing in their fellowship.

Gnosticism

Just as in the book of Acts, outward persecution was not nearly as dangerous as inward error. Perhaps already in the New Testament period, Christians were wrestling against what would eventually be called Gnosticism. The Gnostics were not a unified movement, but rather an assortment of groups that shared some common beliefs. The term *Gnostic* comes from the Greek *gnōsis*, meaning "knowledge"; the Gnostics gave a central role to a secret, deeper understanding of reality. The fundamental Gnostic belief, and the one that Christians could not tolerate, was that all matter was created by an inferior god and thus was basically evil. Liberation from this evil form is the greatest need of every human being, and it must be awakened by receiving the true, hidden knowledge.

Because they rejected matter as evil, Gnostics generally held to the doctrine of Docetism—namely, that Jesus only *appeared* to take on human form. Ignatius wrote against this belief, and Irenaeus and Epiphanius spent substantial energy refuting it. Until the Nag Hammadi Codices were discovered in 1945, nearly the only evidence about the Gnostics was written by their enemies. The discovery of primary sources shows that the Gnostics may not have been an offshoot of Christianity, but rather a development of preexisting Hellenistic Jews who believed that Jesus was the true

God who had appeared to overthrow the wicked Creator and free the souls of mankind.

Although few people today would identify themselves as Gnostic, the tendency to see the physical world as something to escape persists in popular forms of piety. How many funeral services refer to the body as a discarded shell and end with no thought of resurrection? The church fathers described the Gnostics as wildly immoral: If the body is irrelevant, why does it matter what we do? In contrast, the Gnostics described themselves as ascetics: The physical is irrelevant, so do not indulge it. Perhaps both are true. The more intellectual Gnostics emphasized self-denial and focused on the spiritual, while the common people were more prone to decide that their sin was irrelevant. People still fall into both extremes today. The Bible treats both the physical and the spiritual as good creations of God, marred by sin but destined to be restored. Perhaps the most egregious Gnostic error—that there is an evil creator God of the Old Testament from whom Jesus liberates us—is not explicitly taught today, but many Christians treat the first thirty-nine books of the Bible that way. The need for careful theology persists.

Evangelism and Expansion

Though we don't have much reliable data about the places that Christianity spread during this period, there are many legends, such as traditions that Andrew went to Scythia, Thomas to India, and Simon the Zealot to Britain. But there is little firm evidence for these exploits. At the end of the first century, there were perhaps a hundred Christian congregations, mostly in urban areas.[7] It is clearer that the Christians continued to spread out in the regions where they were already present, though their gatherings were still informal. In *Evangelism in the Early Church*, Michael

Green observes that "they did most of their evangelism on what we would call secular ground. You find them in the laundries, at the street corners, and in the wine bars talking about Jesus to all who would listen."[8]

Reaching the world through Jewish and Gentile proselytes was still extremely important; up until the Bar Kokhba rebellion (132–135), all fifteen bishops of the Jerusalem church were ethnic Jews.[9] Though Judaism wasn't popular in the Roman Empire, it held influence disproportionate to its population and provided a bridge into Gentile communities.[10]

Boundaries of the Community

The relationship between Jews and Gentiles remained an important issue during this period. Several heretical groups sought to drive a wedge between the two. The Ebionites believed that Gentiles must submit to the Mosaic law and denied the incarnation of Christ; the Nazoreans believed that ethnically Jewish believers must obey the law; and the Elkesaites rejected the letters of Paul and accepted a book of their founder's prophecies instead.[11] Ignatius emphasized baptism as the entrance into the church, to the extent that he forbade baptism by anyone except the bishop or his designee. In this, we begin to see a clergy/laity distinction that is hard to find in the New Testament.

Discipleship

Ministry in the early churches followed the pattern laid out in Acts 6: Elders focused on the ministry of the Word, and deacons assisted them. However, as early as Ignatius, the concept of a singular bishop of unique authority had begun to develop. Discipleship in this period was especially linked with obeying the spiritual leaders of the community, although there is not yet any reference to doctrines such as apostolic succession, which would dramatically influence later centuries.

In Ignatius's epistle to the Ephesians, he offers an early explanation of the doctrine of Christ: "There is one only physician, of flesh and of spirit, generate and ingenerate, God in man, true Life in death, Son of Mary and Son of God, first passible and then impassible, Jesus Christ our Lord."[12] In this brief paragraph, we see Ignatius wrestling with the Incarnation, the Resurrection, and the Ascension of Christ. Later, in his letter to the Trallians, Ignatius rejected the idea that Jesus only appeared to suffer (the heresy of Docetism) and affirmed Jesus' true humanity.

4

The Apologist Period

(AD 120–AD 220)

In this period, the Christian movement was refined by two sets of fires: heresies within and persecution without. These challenges allowed ideas that previously had simmered beneath the surface to be clarified, and drew lines around the edges of orthodoxy. As new objections to Christianity arose, both from other faiths and from new heresies, the core foundations of theology were refined and sharpened. The Greek word for "defense" is *apologia* (1 Peter 3:15), and thus these defenders of the faith were called apologists. Although this period is comparatively brief, we will examine it at some length because the saints of this era were spiritual giants who shaped everything to come.

Polycarp

The noise in the stadium was chaotic when the prisoner stepped in. Crowned with the silver hair of old age, the man was charged with atheism because he rejected the pagan gods and refused to declare that Caesar was lord. Polycarp (69–155) was the bishop of the church at Smyrna in present-day Turkey, and he had studied with Ignatius and some of Jesus' apostles.

A young man had been tortured earlier that day until he revealed the bishop's location, and the crowd was already on the brink of an ungovernable rage when the proconsul issued a challenge to Polycarp: "Curse Christ and I will free you!"

Polycarp was under no illusions about the proconsul's willingness to harm him. Nevertheless, he stood strong, saying, "Eighty-six years have I served him [Christ], and he has done me no wrong. How can I blaspheme my King and my Savior? . . . I am a Christian. And if you wish to learn what the doctrines of Christianity are, appoint me a day and you shall hear them!"[1]

The proconsul threatened to throw him to the wild animals. Polycarp would not recant. When the proconsul threatened to burn him alive, Polycarp warned him that any fire he set would torment for only a little while, but that the fires of God's judgment were everlasting. As the proconsul ordered him tied to the pyre, Polycarp prayed and thanked God for counting him worthy of martyrdom.

The Martyrdom of Polycarp, which records this story, demonstrates the importance that early Christians placed on faithfulness unto death, following in the steps of Jesus himself. Tradition tells us that Polycarp was a student of the apostle John. It is easy to imagine the aged John, the only one of the twelve to stand at the foot of the cross, telling the young Polycarp about the unimaginable love of Jesus. Perhaps those memories strengthened Polycarp as he faced his own death. When he refused to swear allegiance to the emperor, maybe he was remembering John's admonition: "Dear children, keep yourselves from idols."[2]

Justin Martyr

Polycarp was neither the first nor the last to give his life for the name of Jesus. Perhaps the most important early apologist, Justin, was so closely associated with death for the cause of Christ that "martyr" became his surname. Justin Martyr (100–165) argued against many false teachings, but his most important opponent was Marcion of Sinope (75–155).

Marcion, who rejected all Scripture except the Gospel of Luke and ten of Paul's letters (discounting even some he had edited), believed the creator of the Old Testament was evil, and that Jesus only seemed to take on physical form (Docetism). He is often classified as a Gnostic, though he probably would have rejected the label.[3] Marcion appealed to the anti-Semitism of his contemporaries by offering a clean break with Judaism, and accepting an evil creator both appealed to the philosophy of the day and provided an easy explanation for the problem of evil.

Marcion's heresy spread throughout the Roman Empire, so that Justin could write: "There is a certain Marcion of Pontus, who is even now teaching his disciples to believe in some other god greater than the Demiurge; who by the aid of the demons, has caused many of every race of men and women to speak blasphemies and to deny that God is the Maker of this Universe, and to profess that another, who is greater than He, has done greater works."[4]

Ironically, Marcion did a great service to the orthodox churches. Questions that had simmered beneath the surface were addressed clearly to rebuke his errors. The abiding authority of the Hebrew Scriptures, the unity of God, and the reality of the Incarnation are some of the important doctrines that were refined in response to the Marcionite heresy.

When answering the Marcionites, Justin also challenged

nonbelieving Jews. In his *First Apology* 1.31, he wrote that, although his adversaries read the prophets,

> They do not understand what is said, but consider us enemies and opponents; and like yourselves they kill and punish us whenever they can, as you can well realize. For in the Jewish war which lately happened Bar-Cochba, the leader of the revolt of the Jews, gave orders that Christians alone should be led to terrible punishments, unless they would deny Jesus the Christ and blaspheme. In these books, then, of the prophets we have found it predicted that Jesus our Christ would come, born of a virgin, growing up to manhood, and healing every disease and every sickness and raising the dead, and hated and unrecognized and crucified, and dying and rising again and ascending into heaven, and both being and being called Son of God.[5]

In about AD 96, Emperor Domitian brought a charge of atheism against two relatives of his who were converts to Christianity.[6] This certainly seems like a strange charge: How could Christians be accused of being atheists? Justin explains that they were atheists not because they believed in *no* gods, but because they rejected the pagan pantheon:

> Hence we are called atheists. And we confess that we are atheists with reference to gods such as these, but not with reference to the most true God, the Father of righteousness and temperance and the other virtues, who is unmixed with evil.[7]

Christians were also accused of being cannibals and committing incest, probably due to others misunderstanding the language of Communion and spouses calling each other "brother" and "sister." For advocating the truths of Christian doctrine, Justin gave his life for the gospel (ca. 165) during the reign of Marcus Aurelius.

The Montanists and Tertullian

By the end of the second century, some Christians felt the church had grown cold and lax. Where were the power and zeal of the first generation of Christians? In Phrygia (modern Turkey), a Christian named Montanus was moved by these complaints and believed that God had set him apart as a prophet. The group that gathered around him, originally called the New Prophecy, was very similar to the mainstream church, except for an emphasis on ecstatic prophecy and egalitarianism. Compelling evidence indicates that the early Montanists did not form their own congregations, but were a subculture within the existing churches.

One of the biggest challenges with evaluating the Montanists is that they are known almost entirely through the writings of their enemies. About twenty-five Montanist oracles are recorded by their opponents, but scholars generally consider only about fifteen as genuine.[8] We know that Montanus and two celibate female prophets founded the movement and were buried together, but "if late, clearly fictitious fabrications of a polemical nature to which no scholar has attached any weight are omitted, there is extremely little material one can build upon when one tries to sketch a historical picture of Montanus, Priscilla, and Maximilla."[9]

Because of this, many have wondered whether Montanus was unfairly smeared. John Wesley, whose devotion to personal piety and intimacy with the Holy Spirit parallels what we know of the movement, later wrote, "Nay, I have doubted whether that arch heretic, Montanus, was not one of the holiest men in the second century."[10] Pentecostals have also spoken positively about the Montanists, and people as diverse as Adolf von Harnack and J. M. Carroll have called for a reevaluation of Montanism.[11] Montanists are not unique in having been condemned early in the history of Christianity. Many groups left little mark on history beyond what their enemies wrote about them. As William Tabbernee explains, "Often, as in the case of Montanist writings, material was deliberately destroyed in order to rid the Church of any visible evidence of dissent. This was especially so if dissent was equated with heresy, which almost invariably, it was."[12] When there is little reliable evidence, what we have can sometimes become a Rorschach test where the conclusions say more about the interpreter than the subject.

Other than inscriptions on tombstones or the ruins of buildings (which are difficult to definitively identify as Montanist), the only writings of a Montanist representing himself as such are from Tertullian, who moved from the mainstream church to Montanism toward the end of his life. Even so, scholars are divided on how well Tertullian represents the broader Montanist movement, and how much his influence reshaped their emphases and beliefs.[13] What we can be fairly sure about is that the Montanists gave a prominent role to women in their congregations: There are several Montanist tombs (ca. 200) that identify women as presbyters.[14] Montanists were also devoted to practicing a higher level of piety in a church they felt had cooled. And they believed in an ongoing gift of prophecy, accompanied by ecstatic utterances. Finally, it is likely that the Montanists and the mainstream church did not differ on other major issues, because accusations of doctrinal heresy arose substantially later in church history. Montanists were condemned as heretics in 172, but continued to exist as a dissident group until the sixth century, when "as a final act of defiance during the persecution . . . the last known Montanists burned down their churches on top of themselves."[15]

Tertullian (160–230), the most famous convert to Montanism, wrote more than thirty books after his conversion to Christianity in his thirties. He was widely regarded as one of the greatest intellectuals of his day. Parts of his theology appeal to many evangelicals today. For example, he emphasized a literal interpretation of Scripture over the allegorical approach of many of his peers; he believed in a literal millennial reign when the new Jerusalem would come down out of heaven; he considered the elements of the Eucharist symbolic; and he is responsible for the standard formulation of the Trinity as one substance and three persons. As the first known theologian to use several important words, including *trinity*, he is remembered both for his commitment to holiness and his theological insights. During his Montanist period, he taught that sins were forgiven at baptism and that a person could be forgiven of sin only once post-baptism, in an elaborate, humiliating ritual of penance. Like the Pharisees before him, Tertullian's desire for holiness eventually went beyond what was written and became legalism. Though the Pharisees clung to their traditions and Tertullian sought to eliminate theological gray areas through the New Prophecy, the result was the same. While Tertullian capably argued against Marcion's heretical rejection of the law for grace, he made the opposite error and turned God's grace into a new law. Christians should be humbled that even someone as wise and pious as Tertullian can overreact to the pressures of the day.

Irenaeus

Irenaeus of Lyons (130–202) was Tertullian's peer in intellect, but he had a radically different temperament. His pedigree was impressive: As a young man, he had listened to Polycarp and was therefore a "spiritual grandson" of the apostle John. Irenaeus often lived up to his name (which comes from the Greek word for peace) and argued for the unity of the church. In *Against Heresies*, he gives a beautiful metaphor worth quoting at length:

> As I have already observed, the Church, having received this preaching and this faith, although scattered throughout the whole world, yet, as if occupying but one house, carefully preserves it. She also believes these points [of doctrine] just as if she had but one soul, and one and the same heart, and she proclaims them, and teaches them, and hands them down, with perfect harmony, as if she possessed only one mouth. For, although the languages of the world are dissimilar, yet the import of the tradition is one and the same. . . . But as the sun, that creature of God, is one and the same throughout the whole world, so also the preaching of the truth shineth everywhere, and enlightens all men that are willing to come to a knowledge of the truth. Nor will any one of the rulers in the Churches, however highly gifted he may be in point of eloquence, teach doctrines different from these (for no one is greater than the Master); nor, on the other hand, will he who is deficient in power of expression inflict injury on the tradition. For the faith being ever one and the same, neither does one who is able at great length to discourse regarding it, make any addition to it, nor does one, who can say but little diminish it.[16]

Notice what Irenaeus says and what he doesn't say. On one hand, he emphasizes the unity of the church across the entire world, but he emphasizes a *functional* unity. There is one kind of true church because there is one gospel message, blazing brightly across the whole world. On the other hand, there is no sense of an ecclesiastical hierarchy like that which arose later in Catholic history. Where we might expect a reference to the bishop of Rome or leaders of a diocese, instead the leaders of all of the churches are to teach one and the same thing.

"To illustrate his argument," writes J. N. D. Kelly, "Irenaeus singled out, in a famous and much debated passage, the Roman church; its greatness, its antiquity, its foundation by the apostles Peter and Paul, the fact too that it was universally known, made it an apt example."[17]

The church at Rome does not have authority in and of itself, but as one linked with Peter, Paul, and their eminent successors, it was one that particularly remained faithful. Even this oft-quoted line from *Against Heresies* stands in interesting tension with Ignatius's earlier emphasis on the church gathered around the bishop: "For where the Church is, there is the Spirit of God; and where the Spirit of God is, there is the Church, and every kind of grace; but the Spirit is truth."[18] There is a kind of mutual accountability between churches to a central message: The mark of succession is the Spirit, and the mark of the Spirit is doctrinal fidelity. To Irenaeus, the apostles, prophets, and teachers are the means the Spirit uses to work, so separation from the Church is rejection of the tools God has given us for our good.

Of course, we can see the seeds of the doctrine of apostolic succession that would follow, and the gradual accretion of authority to Rome that would culminate in the office of pope by the fifth century.

There are other areas where most evangelicals would agree with Irenaeus but not with the later development of his thought. He saw Mary as a second Eve, though he did not venerate her; and he understood the elements of Communion to embody spiritual realities, but without affirming the metaphysical complexity of transubstantiation.[19]

One of Irenaeus's greatest legacies is as a biblical theologian. He argued from the books of the Old Testament and also referenced or quoted twenty-three of the twenty-seven books later canonized as the New Testament, emphasizing Jesus as the culmination of God's work in history. By putting Jesus at the center of theology, Irenaeus brought a consistency to biblical interpretation and laid a foundation for the mature reflection of future generations.

What should evangelicals make of Irenaeus's emphasis on the continuity of the church? Does the doctrine of *sola scriptura*, articulated in the Reformation, inevitably fall into the same trap as the Gnostics and the Montanists? There is an important distinction. Gnostics (like some cults today) believed they could go beyond the Scripture to some new authority that could correct the revealed message of God. The Protestant Reformers, on the other hand, sought to turn the leaders of the church back to the truth the apostles had taught, thereby restoring biblical truth. Still, we should humbly consider the dangers of well-meaning Christians developing their own beliefs apart from involvement in a faithful community. Even Martin Luther posting his Ninety-Five Theses shows that he intended to have a conversation within the broader family of God, rather than develop ideas on his own. Our brothers and sisters in the faith, whether living or dead, are not infallible, but they are valuable.

The Antiochians and Alexandrians

In the early centuries of the church, there were two great schools, in both senses of the word. Alexandria and Antioch both offered formal instruction, but also represented two schools of thought in their approach to the Bible. The Antiochian school emphasized a literal understanding of Scripture and produced the famous preacher John Chrysostom. Unfortunately, the Nestorian controversy (chapter 6) also arose from Antioch, tarnishing the reputation of the Antiochian school. The Alexandrians emphasized a spiritual and allegorical interpretation of Scripture, and were influenced by Plato's philosophical ideas.

Clement of Alexandria (150–215), not to be confused with the earlier Clement of Rome, was an educated man who studied under the famous philosopher Pantaenus. He eventually became a Christian and an ardent apologist for Christianity. Clement's major work is *Stromateis*, or *Miscellanies*. Divided into eight books, *Stromateis* contains an attack on paganism and a defense of Christianity; an extensive discussion of Christian ethics; an examination of Gnosticism, a topic of great interest to Clement; the role of philosophy in the Christian life; and a discussion of the Old Testament that demonstrates the Alexandrian approach. The seventh book is interesting to historians for its insights on baptism and the Lord's Supper.

Another important theologian, though one who is more difficult to evaluate, is Origen of Alexandria (185–254). Origen was one of the most prolific writers of the early church, and his works cover a wide range of topics. Unfortunately, many of Origen's works have been lost, and those that remain are often fragmentary. Educated in both Christian and pagan thought, Origen became one of the most respected biblical scholars of his day. He was heavily influenced by Plato, and this is evident in his writings. Origen was an important figure in the development of early Christian theology. He was one of the first to explore the idea of the Trinity, and he wrote extensively on topics such as the nature of Christ, the role of Scripture, and the nature of God. Even in his own lifetime, Origen was controversial, and many of his speculations will strike evangelicals as bizarre, but his influence and intellect cannot be doubted.

Evangelism and Expansion

As Christians began to engage more deliberately with pagan intellectuals, they would have understood that for many of the important Hellenist leaders, "it was not necessary that people should *believe in* the ancient gods. Belief was a private matter. But they were expected to participate in the state cult. Worship was a public matter, and the safety of the state depended upon it."[20] That may be one reason that the Romans found the refusal of Christians to swear allegiance to Caesar or offer a pinch of incense to him so bizarre. You don't have to *believe* it, but what's the harm in performing the sacrifices for the sake of the nation?

Also, the peers of the early Christians did not think that religion determined ethics. The two key pillars of Christian conversion, *faith* and *repentance*, were alien to the Greco-Roman world. Moreover, the exclusivity of Christian worship (like Jewish worship before it) simply didn't make sense in a polytheistic society. Before people could be expected to convert to Christianity, the apologists had the heavy task of creating an intellectual environment in which conversion was comprehensible.

But they took on this task with boldness, both among the intelligentsia and along normal social lines. Timothy George powerfully describes the evangelistic zeal of the first centuries of Christianity: "They went everywhere—into the arenas, the academies of learning, the marketplace, to faraway lands such as India and Ethiopia, into every nook and cranny of the Roman Empire."[21] Rome's roads and rivers provided natural venues for the gospel to travel, and the apologists planted seeds that would continue to grow. By the end of this period, Tertullian could say,

> We are but of yesterday, and we have filled every place among you—cities, islands, fortresses, towns, market-places, the very camp, tribes, companies, palace, senate, forum—we have left nothing to you but the temples of your gods. For what wars should we not be fit, not eager, even with unequal forces, we who so willingly yield ourselves to the sword, if in our religion it were not counted better to be slain than to slay.[22]

Boundaries of the Community

In response to heretics like Marcion, the Apologists argued that the true church had an unbroken line of leaders going back to the apostles themselves. This concept eventually evolved into apostolic succession. The community is defined in this era by continuity, with the church as a conservative institution, passing on the truths entrusted to her by God. Baptism, as in all ages of Christianity, is the basic entrance point to the community. Tertullian, with his usual rigidity, believed that baptism removed sin and that the forgiveness of serious sin post-baptism was only possible once. For him and many others, the boundary of the community was abso-lute faithfulness. For the mainstream churches, there was much more tolerance for error. Churches still fall into these two extremes today, and the balance of holiness and grace continues to challenge believers.

Discipleship

How should the Bible be interpreted? The Antiochian and Alexandrian schools handled their discipleship differently because they differed on the nature of Scripture. Was it a literal text to be understood directly, or was it primarily something to be mined for deeper meaning through allegorical reflection? This distinction is obviously too simple: Both schools included elements of both approaches, but their emphases were radically different. Tertullian's focus on the literal sense of Scripture may have contributed toward his legalism, but it also made him a brilliant theologian responsible for coining the word *Trinity*.

As the Christians of the Apologist era interacted with the surrounding community, they continued to face the challenge of how to be *in* the world but not *of* it. Despite the protests of some, the leading thinkers of this age employed Greek philosophy to engage with Greek philosophers. Importantly, they discussed Christ as the true Logos, a term common in Greek philosophy and used—but not fully developed—in the Gospel of John.

5

Conflict with the Empire

(AD 220–AD 305)

THE MOOD MUST HAVE BEEN SOMBER in January 250. The Roman
Empire was in deep crisis. Decius, who had been emperor for less
than a year, issued a proclamation that everyone across the empire
must choose between publicly offering a sacrifice to the pagan
gods or being put to death. Many believers chose martyrdom,
and Decius was happy to oblige. Although Christians had been
persecuted occasionally throughout the history of the church, the
era of conflict was marked by an intensification of attacks. Decius
and Diocletian launched a wave of hostility toward Christianity
that was widespread and intense. Humanly speaking, this persecution might have demolished the Christian movement. Instead,
Tertullian's famous words were fulfilled and the blood of the martyrs became the seed of the church.

Public Churches

Dura was a short-lived Roman colony, controlled by the Parthians until 211 and conquered by the Sassanids in 256. After that, the city was abandoned and buried by the sands of time, which preserved it until soldiers accidentally discovered it in 1931. When the ruins were excavated in 1932 and 1933, the brief Roman occupation provided staggering insights into the early days of Christianity. A home was discovered that had been modified into a dedicated meeting place for the church there. Pagan art was plastered over, tiles and benches had been added, and a platform had been built in one of the rooms along with seating for one hundred people.[1] One room, probably a storage room, had been converted into a baptistry, complete with a font and a basin large enough to immerse an adult. Because Christianity was still illegal, the exterior of the building had been changed only modestly, but the policy of not seeking out Christians remained in force, and meeting together was apparently a risk the people were willing to take.[2]

Perhaps churches had repurposed buildings even earlier: Tertullian mentioned the doors of the church in his *On Modesty*, and the *Syriac Edessene Chronicle* records the destruction of "the temple of the church of the Christians" in 201.[3] Porphyry mocks believers in *Against the Christians*, but he provides valuable insight when he mentions that, "imitating the construction of temples, [they] erect great buildings in which they meet to pray, though there is nothing to prevent them from doing this in their own homes since, of course, their Lord hears them everywhere."[4] The church historian Eusebius confirms that Christians, by this point, "not content with the ancient buildings . . . erected spacious churches from the foundation in all the cities."[5] Christians began to enjoy comfortable and, at least sometimes, prosperous lives, and their worship reflected those privileges.

The Old Roman Creed

As church facilities were becoming more organized and well structured, Christians continued to develop their theology as well. From the earliest times, converts apparently confessed their faith at their baptism, in response to questions. At some point, this was crystallized into a "declaratory creed":

> I believe in God the Father almighty;
> and in Christ Jesus His only Son, our Lord,
> Who was born from the Holy Spirit and the Virgin Mary,
> Who under Pontius Pilate was crucified, and buried,
> on the third day rose again from the dead,
> ascended to heaven,
> sits on the right hand of the Father,
> whence he will come to judge the living and the dead;
> and in the Holy Spirit, the holy Church, the remission of sins,
> the resurrection of the flesh.[6]

The basic structure matches the baptismal formula from Matthew 28 (Father, Son, and Holy Spirit), a pattern followed by many early creeds. By the fifth century, this developed into what is today called the Apostles' Creed. Though not entirely, the changes are mostly expansions of the existing language (for example, "I believe in God the Father almighty" becomes "I believe in God the Father almighty, creator of heaven and earth"). It is encouraging to realize that the core of the faith is not new; these basic tenets have been upheld for nearly two thousand years.

Major Persecution

By the time Severus Alexander took the throne in 222, the stability that Rome had experienced under Augustus and his successors was long forgotten. Severus ascended to replace his recently assassinated cousin, who was only eighteen years old. Severus was even younger, and by the time he was killed in 235, at the age of twenty-six, he had been in power almost half his life. With his death, the empire was plunged into chaos, which did not subside until the bloody reign of Diocletian (284–305). Severus was sympathetic to Christianity and reportedly included a statue of Jesus among other gods in his private temple. He provides a good example of the way many outsiders apparently thought of Christianity at the time: an interesting trinket, maybe one to be eventually assimilated with the rest.

Severus is interesting by contrast to Decius, who reigned from 249 to 251. Decius was the first emperor to try to exterminate Christianity across the entire Roman Empire. Some leaders were killed immediately, while others were given a chance to recant their Christianity. Like Polycarp before them, all they had to do was offer a small sacrifice or burn a little incense and they would be spared. Tragically, many complied and were given certificates that they had passed the test of loyalty to Rome. Others bribed Roman officials to gain the tickets without actually performing the sacrifices. Perhaps the suddenness of the persecution overwhelmed them. Perhaps they offered the same justification that many might offer today: Can't I do much more for God alive than dead? Regardless of the reason, churches across the empire lost many from among their flocks, through both faithfulness and faithlessness. A few months before the end of Decius's short reign, the persecution stopped, but the reprieve was only temporary.

Diocletian rose to power when Rome was on the brink of collapse. In every way, the empire was fragile and in need of a strong hand—which Diocletian provided. During the bulk of his reign, Christians benefited from the prosperity and security he provided.

Eusebius's *Church History* testifies to the favor and respect that Christians were given—though he also notes the laxity brought on by comfort.

In 302, Diocletian changed course, apparently believing that devotion to the Roman gods was now essential for national prosperity. He sought to reunify the empire under the traditional pantheon by issuing four edicts.

First, he called for the destruction of public places of worship, banned the assembling of Christians, and burned the Scriptures. Next, he imprisoned all clergy. The third edict allowed the clergymen to be released if they would sacrifice to the Roman gods. The final edict required all Christians, clergy or otherwise, to offer sacrifices.

Eusebius, a young man at the time, describes the persecution and its aftermath in his *Ecclesiastical History*:

> It was the nineteenth year of the reign of Diocletian and
> the month of Dystrus, called by the Romans March, in
> which the festival of our Saviour's passion was at hand,
> when the imperial edicts were everywhere published
> to tear down the churches to their foundations, and to
> destroy the sacred Scriptures by fire. They commanded,
> also, that those who were in honorable stations should
> be degraded and those who were freedmen should
> be deprived of their liberty if they persevered in their
> adherence to Christianity.
>
> . . . The first edict against us was of this nature, but
> it was not long before other edicts were also issued, in
> which it was ordered that all the prelates in every place
> should first be committed to prison, and then, by every
> artifice, constrained to offer sacrifice to the gods. . . .

Vast numbers of the prelates of the church endured with a noble resolution the most appalling trials and exhibited instances of illustrious conflicts for the faith. Vast numbers, however, of others, broken and relaxed in spirit by timidity before the contest, voluntarily yielded at the first onset. But of the rest, each encountered various kinds of torments. Here was one who was scourged with rods, there another tormented with the rack and excruciating scrapings, in which some at the time endured the most terrible death. . . . Here one, taken up when half dead, was thrown out as if he were already dead; . . . there another, lying upon the ground, was dragged a long distance by the feet and numbered among those who had sacrificed. One, however, would cry out, and with a loud voice declared his abhorrence of the sacrifice. Another exclaimed that he was a Christian, furnishing by confession an illustrious example of this salutary name. Another asserted that he neither had sacrificed nor intended to sacrifice; . . . but these were forced to silence by numerous bands of soldiers prepared for this purpose, by whom they were struck on the face and cheeks and violently driven away.

Thus the enemies of religion, upon the whole, deemed it a great matter even to appear to have gained some advantage. But these things did not avail them much against the saints. No description could suffice to give an exact account of their courage.[7]

Christians responded to this persecution in much the same way that they had endured the early wave of persecution under Decius. Some complied, some lied, and some died. Those who gave their lives were honored, but those who offered sacrifices (or claimed to) and later wanted to return to the fellowship of the church created a sticky issue that persisted into the next century (see the Donatist Controversy in chapter 6). How can those who betrayed the faith to save their lives be accepted back? Didn't that dishonor those who had endured unto death? There was plenty of time to wrestle with these issues, because although the persecution ebbed and flowed, it continued for about a decade, until the reign of Constantine.

Evangelism and Expansion

By the end of this period of conflict, the gospel had spread to every part of the Roman Empire and as far as Germany and Britain. Increasingly intense persecution did not prevent the spread of the gospel, but instead advanced it. The most obvious means that God used to take what was meant for evil and use it for good was the testimony of the Christians who persevered in their faithfulness, even to the point of death. There was a magnetism to such a sincere belief that even the danger of coming to Christ could not overcome. Then, as now, one of the greatest aids to the advancement of the Christian faith is sincerity and faithfulness.

Boundaries of the Community

The Old Roman Creed provided an important set of boundaries around what it meant to be a Christian, and it probably was initially rooted in the questions asked at baptism. The process of baptism was complex. Those who wanted to be baptized would first go through a lengthy period of instruction, followed by a time of separation and fasting before the baptism itself, which usually took place around Easter. The candidates would publicly confess their faith, and apparently the usual custom was to immerse them three times in running water. According to the Didache, other methods of immersion could be used, and even pouring water over the believer was allowed in extreme circumstances. Hermas, Justin Martyr, Tertullian, and Cyprian all connect baptism with the new birth and consider it the entryway to Christian community.

Another boundary is also important and uniquely tied to this period: Christians were defined by what they would not do. If worshipers were willing to offer incense to Zeus, it didn't mean they had no special affinity for Hera, but it did mean they had no relationship with Christ. The church consisted of those who were devoted to Christ alone, who recognized his work in history and the future. The question of whether those who had apostatized could be received again remained unsettled during the time of persecution, but it certainly lingered in the background.

Discipleship

For doctrinal instruction, the Old Roman Creed was also an important model. It outlined the basics of the faith in a memorable, organized way in a world where many converts were functionally illiterate. Another important document, although less certainly sourced, is *Apostolic Tradition*, attributed to the martyr Hippolytus. It lays out practical steps for various church functions, along with important insights into the understanding of discipleship in the third century. For example, it includes guidelines about which professions a Christian must give up: both obvious ones, such as prostitution or overseeing gladiatorial matches as a public official; and more surprising ones, like acting or driving a chariot. It also includes instructions on the importance of giving thanks for all food, praying before beginning the day's work, being on time when the Word of God was preached, and so on.

There is an important tension here that Christians continue to face. On the one hand, the accumulation of the oral law around the law of Moses was a continual frustration for Jesus and the apostles. People wanted to adhere to what God had said and eliminate any ambiguity. It is difficult to read a document like the *Apostolic Tradition* without sensing this impulse: The number of prayers per day is described in detail, with instructions about going into another room if your spouse is unbaptized. On the other hand, discipleship must be practical. There is a need to teach people to pray over their meals, to avoid situations that compromise sexual purity, and to evaluate whether or not a particular career honors God. As our study continues, we will see this conflict between liberty and clarity raise its head repeatedly. Thankfully, the words of James 1:5 still hold true: "If you need wisdom, ask our generous God, and he will give it to you. He will not rebuke you for asking."

6

The Empire Period

(AD 305–AD 476)

IN ABOUT 390, EMPEROR THEODOSIUS ordered a massacre in the historic city of Thessalonica, killing seven thousand people in three hours. Ambrose, bishop of Milan, sent a letter to the emperor, barring him from receiving the Eucharist until he humbled himself and repented. His message to the Byzantine emperor is stunning:

> I have written this, not in order to confound you, but
> that the examples of these kings [David and Saul] may
> stir you up to put away this sin from your kingdom, for
> you will do it away by humbling your soul before God.
> You are a man, and it has come upon you, conquer it.
> Sin is not done away but by tears and penitence. Neither
> angel can do it, nor archangel. The Lord Himself, Who
> alone can say, "I am with you," if we have sinned, does
> not forgive any but those who repent.[1]

Even more amazing is that Theodosius accepted the humiliation that Ambrose demanded. In front of the congregation, he removed his beautiful imperial robes and asked for forgiveness. He was required to do this on several occasions before he was finally restored.

At the beginning of the fourth century, 5 to 10 percent of the population of Rome were Christians.[2] Not only had persecution not extinguished their faith, but it had provided opportunities to display their faith, which drew more and more people into the church. Yet, no one could have predicted that, within one hundred years, Rome would be sacked and the power of Christianity unrivaled throughout the known world.

The Donatist Controversy

During the bloody persecution of the 200s, many Christians had denied their faith to save their lives. Those who had relapsed into heathenism were called *lapsi*, which included *traditores*, who were "Christians (mostly clerics) who . . . gave up the sacred books to the authorities."[3] Once the persecution was over, could they be restored? Were they damned? Did they occupy some middle ground, forgiven by God but never readmitted to the church? The issue of serious sin was a major conflict in the earlier Montanist movement, with Tertullian striking a hard line against Callistus, the bishop of Rome at the time, arguing that there was no room for forgiving murderers, adulterers, or apostates.

Cyprian (210–258) was the bishop of Carthage, and though he had not denied the faith, he had gone into hiding during the great persecution of Decius. Rigorists, such as the Roman theologian Novatian (200–258), said that such sins could never be forgiven. On the opposite extreme, some believed that those who had not succumbed to torture had earned a special level of favor with God and that their merit could be extended. Cyprian rejected both paths, proposing a complex system of repentance based on the circumstances of the sin. Thus, the third Catholic sacrament (after baptism and the Lord's Supper) was born: *penance*.

Predictably, this lenience led to the development of a stricter faction. The Donatists rejected the idea that those who had abandoned the faith could be restored, no matter what their level of repentance. They broke away from the Catholic Church and elected their own bishops, rejecting the lapsed priests and rebaptizing their converts.

Who is properly authorized to baptize? For some people, this might become an eminently practical question. If the person who performed your baptism later abandons the faith or declares they were never born again in the first place, do you need to be rebaptized? Or does the validity of the baptism rest in the sincerity of the candidate? Cyprian argued that the authority for baptism rests in the church, not the bishop or the candidate (*Epistle* 69.7). Augustine later made the same point: The authority was Christ's; the quality of the mediator was not essential.

Though some claimed that the "one baptism" mentioned in Ephesians 4:5 meant that baptisms performed by heretics should be accepted, Cyprian argued that converts were not being rebaptized, but baptized by proper authority for the first time.[4] The Donatists held the same view in reverse: They were not rebaptizing former Catholics, but properly baptizing those who had been baptized by illegitimate priests.

The fundamental issue was the nature of the church. Should it be a pure assembly of saints, radically different from the world around it? Or a hospital for sinners, a mixed multitude of the genuinely born again and superficial professors, like the wheat and the tares in Matthew 13:24-43? This dispute might have ended in some kind of compromise, but everything was about to change when Christianity began to merge with the empire.

A New Kind of Emperor

Diocletian, struggling with poor health, retired in 305 with a succession plan in place to reward his friends and relatives with positions of power. He had developed the idea of a tetrarchy, a two-tiered system of government with two emperors at the top called Augustus (one in the East and one in the West) and their successors and assistants called Caesars. The plan was doomed to failure. Constantinus was promoted from Caesar to Augustus but died within a year. His son Constantine, a capable military commander, was proclaimed Augustus by his troops in his father's place, contrary to the established plan. Gradually, Constantine established dominance over his enemies, defeating them in battle, forcing their suicides, or simply outliving them. Eventually, in 324, the East and West were reunited under Constantine as the sole emperor.

Early in his reign, Constantine the Great (272–337) called for an end to the persecution of Christians in the western empire; but in the eastern empire, efforts to stamp out Christianity increased. Emperor Galerius offered an official Edict of Toleration in the East in 311, only when it was obvious that his extermination efforts had failed, and he died shortly thereafter. This edict formally pardoned Christians for the "crime" of failing to worship the Roman gods, with one condition: "Wherefore, for this our indulgence, they ought to pray to their God for our safety, for that of the republic, and for their own, that the republic may continue uninjured on every side, and that they may be able to live securely in their homes."[5]

The most interesting thing about Constantine was not his

toleration of Christianity, but his ostensible conversion in 312, after a battle against Maxentius near Rome. According to tradition, Constantine had a vision of a flaming cross in the sky and heard the words, "In this sign you will conquer." He put this vision to the test at the Battle of Milvian Bridge, ordering his troops to paint the Chi-Rho (a monogram made from the first two letters of *Christ*) on their shields. Constantine's victory was decisive, and he credited his victory to Jesus.

Perhaps *convert* is too generous a word. Constantine remained high priest of the pagan Roman religion, wasn't baptized until he was on his deathbed, and kept his public comments ambiguous. Church historians such as Eusebius saw him as a new David, bringing peace to God's people. Others feared that collusion with the empire would lead to corruption and disaster. Still, when Maximinus Daia resumed persecution in the East despite the Edict of Toleration, Constantine and Licinius allied together to defeat him and issued the Edict of Milan (313), which provided official toleration for Christians throughout the empire. The edict did not make Christianity the state religion, but it put an end to the persecution of Christians. But when Licinius took control of the East in 320, he began persecuting the Christians again, before finally being defeated by Constantine, who found that his political ambitions and professed religion conveniently aligned as he became the sole emperor.

Although Christianity did not become the official religion of Rome until the reign of Theodosius I (379–395), who issued the Edict of Thessalonica in February 380, Constantine built expensive structures on important Christian sites and favored the religion throughout the empire.

This transition from a persecuted minority to a pampered, favored faith was not without its consequences. Instead of a genuine faith bringing people to profess Christ, there was now a social pressure to conform. Speaking out against the sins of the powerful is one thing when they are your enemy. It takes a different type of courage to speak against them, as Ambrose did, when you enjoy privileges they can take away.

Different emperors treated the faith differently, from Julian's attempted return to paganism to Theodosius's willingness to repent publicly when he sinned. But the overall trajectory was set. By 391, pagan sacrifices were the ones that were banned, and pagan temples were destroyed by Christian mobs. When imperial money was withdrawn, paganism as a movement collapsed. Though some pagans practiced a modified version of their traditions until the early sixth century, their numbers were few and their worship bore little resemblance to that of their predecessors.[6]

Ecumenical Councils

Now connected with the Roman government, the churches began to develop a more organized hierarchy. One way this was manifested was through ecumenical councils, also called general councils. These meetings were convened by the emperor and theoretically represented all orthodox Christians.

When Christianity became a national concern instead of merely a private one, doctrinal disputes affected the unity of the empire. For Christianity to be what Constantine desired, and what the bishops surely would have argued it should be by Christ's design, there was a need for unity. The tool of that unity became a succession of creeds.

The first council, and perhaps the most important, the First Council of Nicaea, centered on one basic question: Who is Jesus? On July 14, 325, about three hundred bishops and deacons met together with the emperor, who told them solemnly that a divided church was worse than war.[7] The division in the group was seemingly arcane: Was Jesus of the same essence (ὁμοούσιος) as the Father or merely of a similar essence (ὁμοιούσιος) as the Father? Those uninterested in theology might balk at the idea that a single letter could be worth dividing over. But one word meant that Jesus was the eternal God himself made flesh, and the other meant that he was a god but a created one, not the ultimate Creator. The latter view was pushed by an influential theologian from Antioch named Arius (250–336) and is called Arianism. On the opposite side of the debate was Athanasius (296–373), who argued forcefully that there was never a time when Jesus did not exist, and that he is truly God. Athanasius prevailed, and the Nicene Christology took the force of law:

We believe in one God, the Father Almighty, maker of all things visible and invisible; and in one Lord Jesus Christ, the Son of God, the only begotten of his Father, of the substance of the Father, God of God, Light of Light, very God of very God, begotten, not made, being of one substance with the Father. By whom all things were made, both which be in heaven and in earth. Who for us men and for our salvation came down [from heaven] and was incarnate and was made man. He suffered and the third day he rose again, and ascended into heaven. And he shall come again to judge both the quick and the dead. And [we believe] in the Holy Ghost. And whosoever shall say that there was a time when the Son of God was not, or that before he was begotten he was not, or that he was made of things that were not, or that he is of a different substance or essence [from the Father] or that he is a creature, or subject to change or conversion—all that so say, the Catholic and Apostolic Church anathematizes them.[8]

The First Council of Constantinople (381) is less aptly called an ecumenical council; it consisted of only 150 Eastern (Greek-speaking) bishops with no one from the Western (Latin) empire present—not even the bishop of Rome was invited.[9] It reaffirmed Nicaea and condemned Apollinarianism, a heresy claiming that the divine Logos replaced the human soul of Jesus so that he was not fully human. From a practical point of view, it is interesting that the third canon (or rule of faith) declares that the bishop of Constantinople is second in prestige only to Rome, as the city was the new Rome (the capital of the empire). Certainly that canon was easier to pass without any Western representatives. The sixth canon of Nicaea discussed the authority of metropolitan bishops over their regions, with Rome listed as an example but not as superior to the others. At this point, it seems that the pope did not have a well-established authority over the whole of Christendom. The creed commonly known as the Nicene Creed is connected with Constantinople, though it may not have been prepared there.[10]

The First Council of Ephesus (431) built on the proclamations of the previous two councils. Nicaea protected the divinity of Christ, and Constantinople protected the humanity of Christ, but the mystery of how these two were connected remained to be clarified.

Nestorius, bishop of Constantinople, was uncomfortable with the idea of calling Mary "the mother of God" (literally, "God bearer") and preferred "the mother of Christ." He believed that Christ was fully human and fully divine, but that his natures were separable and that Mary could only be properly called the mother of his humanity. The council declared this point of view anathema, and Nestorius resigned without defending himself.

Many modern scholars question whether Nestorius actually divided the person of Christ in the way he was accused. The entire proceedings were steeped in politics, and the evidence that survives is not at all clear. But whether the condemnations were accurate or not, the heresy of Nestorianism has borne his name ever since, and the sect continues to the present day. The bishops at Ephesus also condemned Pelagianism, which we will discuss below.

The Council of Chalcedon (451) was accepted by both the Roman Catholic and Eastern Orthodox churches, but the canon laws were rejected by Rome. Like the previous ecumenical councils, the vast majority of the more than five hundred bishops present were from the Eastern churches, with only four attending from the West. The Roman Catholic Church objected to Canon 28, which reaffirmed the declaration from Ephesus that the Roman bishop's authority came from the political structure of the empire, and that Constantinople was equal in privilege and second in prestige. If the council, though almost entirely Greek, was willing to approve this canon, clearly the pope's authority was not a settled matter.

Much more important is the council's brilliant summation of the doctrine of the hypostatic union (how Christ can be both fully human and fully divine). The question they faced was still the same: Who is Jesus? Nicaea had confirmed that he was fully God, of the same essence as the Father. At Constantinople, the council confirmed that he was fully man, with no part of his humanity supplanted by divinity. The Council of Ephesus had argued that Christ's natures were inseparable, but since then a new group, called Monophysites, claimed that Christ had only one nature. Clear language was needed to respond to this overreaction, while continuing to affirm the claims of the past. Thus the Chalcedonian Creed was affirmed.

> In agreement, therefore, with the holy fathers, we all unanimously teach that we should confess that our Lord Jesus Christ is one and the same Son, the same perfect in Godhead and the same perfect in manhood, truly God and truly man, *the same of a rational soul and body, consubstantial with the Father in Godhead, and the same consubstantial with us in manhood, like us in all things except sin*; begotten from the Father before the ages as regards His Godhead, and in the last days, the same, because of us and because of our salvation begotten from the Virgin Mary, the *Theotokos*, as regards His manhood; one and the same Christ, Son, Lord, only-begotten, *made known in two natures without confusion, without change, without division, without separation*, the difference of the natures being by no means removed because of the union, but the property of each nature being preserved and coalescing in one *prosopon* and *one hupostasis—not parted or divided into two prosopa, but one and the same Son, only-begotten, divine Word, the Lord Jesus Christ*, as the prophets of old and Jesus Christ Himself have taught us about Him and the creed of our fathers has handed down.[11]

This formulation is rejected by the Armenian, Coptic, Ethiopian, and Syrian Orthodox churches, which remain separate groups today. They deny the charge of Monophysite theology and prefer the term Miaphysitism. Both sides sought to emphasize the trueness of Christ's divinity and humanity, though the Monophysites effectively taught that Christ's humanity and divinity combined to create some new, third type of entity. Perhaps the most important takeaway from this is that what might have appeared to be minor and theoretical distinctions in generations before and after the councils were issues of intense deliberation during the Empire period. There was a focus on standardization as a means of uniting the empire, which sometimes caused division instead.

The Canon of Scripture

A key example of standardization was the clarification of the canon of Scripture. The word *canon* referred originally to a measuring ruler or other fixed standard, but it usually has the derivative meaning of an authoritative set of texts. In church history it refers to the books that have been identified as true Scripture. Keep in mind that as early as Marcion (75–155), the contents of the Bible were disputed. In response to the Marcionite heresy, orthodox Christians reaffirmed their acceptance of the Hebrew Old Testament. After all, Jesus told his disciples to do what the Pharisees said, even as he warned against their hypocrisy (Matthew 23:1-3). But how was the New Testament formed? A fragment of a list of authoritative books (called the Muratorian Canon after L. A. Muratori, who discovered it) may date to AD 200, but it is difficult to be certain. Many scholars now date it around 400. The document, which is damaged at the beginning and the end, begins:

> . . . but at some he was present, and so he set them down.
> The third book of the Gospel, that according to Luke,
> was compiled in his own name on Paul's authority by
> Luke the physician, when after Christ's ascension Paul
> had taken him to be with him like a legal expert. Yet
> neither did *he* see the Lord in the flesh; and he too, as

he was able to ascertain events, begins his story from the birth of John.

The fourth of the Gospels was written by John, one of the disciples. When exhorted by his fellow-disciples and bishops, he said, "Fast with me this day for three days; and what may be revealed to any of us, let us relate it to one another." The same night it was revealed to Andrew, one of the apostles, that John was to write all things in his own name, and they were all to certify.[12]

Clearly, the lost part of the text refers to the Gospels of Matthew and Mark, but the descriptions are useful for understanding the criteria the church used to identify the authoritative books of Scripture: *apostolicity*, *catholicity*, and *orthodoxy*.

Apostolicity means that the books must be traceable back to the apostles or their close associates. The Gospel of Luke is explicitly tied to Paul's authority, though Luke wrote it. The Gospel of John was written by the disciple of Jesus, and the other surviving apostles verified what he had written. The next section of the Muratorian fragment helps us understand the other two criteria:

Therefore, though various ideas are taught in the several books of the Gospels, yet it makes no difference to the faith of believers, since by one sovereign Spirit all things are declared in all of them concerning the Nativity, the Passion, the Resurrection, the conversation with his disciples and his two comings, the first in lowliness and contempt, which has come to pass, the second glorious with royal power, which is to come.

What marvel therefore if John so firmly sets forth each statement in his Epistles too, saying of himself, *What*

*we have seen with our eyes and heard with our ears and our
hands have handled, these things we have written to you?*
For so he declares himself not an eyewitness and a hearer
only, but a writer of all the marvels of the Lord in order.[13]

Catholicity refers to the applicability of the books to all believers. We know for certain that the apostles wrote documents that
are lost to us (see 1 Corinthians 5:9), but apparently the missing
letters were not intended for future generations.

Orthodoxy is faithfulness to what God had previously revealed
(Galatians 1:8). The defense of the four Gospels touches on both
points: They all present the gospel and they all accord with what
God has revealed.[14]

In addition to the Gospels, the fragment lists Acts, the seven
church letters of Paul (emphasizing catholicity: "yet *one* Church
is recognized as being spread over the entire world"[15]), Philemon,
Titus, 1 and 2 Timothy, Jude, "the couple bearing the name of
John, [and] . . . the Apocalypse also of John, and of Peter."[16] The
language about Peter is confusing, referring to the *Apocalypse of
Peter* or one of his letters; in either case, the fragment notes that
the authority of that book was disputed. It is unclear which two
of John's letters are intended, and Hebrews and James are missing entirely, though perhaps, like Matthew and Mark, they were
included on a lost part of the document.

The *Wisdom of Solomon* and the *Shepherd of Hermas* are listed
as commonly read, but the *Wisdom of Solomon* is described as
being pseudonymous, and *Hermas* is identified as a recent book,
inappropriate for reading in the church. Several other books are
rejected as being heretical.

Eusebius offers his own canon list in chapter 25 of *Church
History*. As a historian, he is not attempting to establish his own

canon list, but to report what was commonly accepted at the time. He includes the Gospels, Acts, the letters of Paul, 1 John, and 1 Peter as universally accepted. The Revelation of John was nearly universally accepted in the West, and Eusebius lists it among the accepted books; but he doubted John's authorship, so he hedges his comments. James, 2 Peter, and 2 and 3 John are listed as disputed books. Revelation was more disputed in the East, whereas Hebrews was accepted there as among the letters of Paul.

In an era before the printing press and when churches were still independent of a central authority, it should not be surprising that the acceptance of a common canon was a gradual process. A consensus formed around which books met the criteria of apostolicity, catholicity, and orthodoxy, which was then recognized by councils and creeds. By 367, Athanasius listed the New Testament canon that we use today with the addition of some other books that he believed were helpful but not authoritative, such as *The Wisdom of Solomon*, the Didache, and the *Shepherd of Hermas*. The Syriac churches (i.e., those under the bishop of Antioch) were slower to agree, not adding 2 Peter, 2 and 3 John, Jude, and Revelation until the sixth century.

The Doctors of the Church

Christians have traditionally identified four great "doctors" of the church, in the older sense of the word, meaning teacher. These theologians left an impact far beyond their lifetimes, and three of them lived during the Empire period. The fourth, Gregory the Great, will be discussed in another chapter.

Ambrose (340–397), from what is now Trier in modern Germany, became bishop of Milan. He was one of the most influential of the Latin church fathers, though he was not a theological innovator. Instead, he was primarily a pastor, whose concerns were practical. The bulk of his writings are transcriptions of sermons he preached, and they address moral issues facing his congregation.

The second great doctor was Augustine (354–430), from Thagaste in North Africa. Raised by a devout Christian mother named Monica, but enamored of sexual immorality and convinced that Christianity was for the weak-minded, Augustine was an unlikely candidate for being considered the most important theologian in history. Augustine met Ambrose, whose example persuaded him that Christianity could be intellectual, but it wasn't until Augustine heard a child singing, "Take and read," that he opened the Bible to Romans 13:13-14 and came to faith. Ambrose baptized him the following Easter, and Augustine soon rose to great respect and prominence—involving himself in every major theological conflict that arose during his lifetime. His hundreds of written works include *The City of God*, a massive apologetic in response to the sack of Rome by the Visigoths in 410, and *Confessions*, his autobiography.

One of Augustine's most important contributions to Christian theology was his controversy with Pelagius (390–418), a British theologian who apparently denied the doctrine of original sin. Original sin, as taught by Augustine, is the idea that the guilt of Adam has corrupted human beings completely, so that apart from the grace of God we stand condemned. We have frustratingly poor evidence for what Pelagius actually believed, compared to what his enemies said he believed and what his followers later taught, but the movement that bears his name taught that human will is completely free and that people can be saved by their own merit.

Jerome (347–420), the third great doctor of the church, was born in Stridon, a village on the border of Dalmatia and Pannonia, an area now divided among several Balkan states. He is best known for translating the Bible into Latin. This translation, known as the

Vulgate, had a profound impact on the development of Western Christianity and was the authoritative Bible for almost every Christian for about a thousand years. Even when the Bible was first translated into the common vernacular, early translations were dependent on the Latin Vulgate. Jerome also wrote a number of important theological works, including commentaries on the Bible and treatises on Christian doctrine.

The Papacy

It is fascinating to observe the gradual consolidation of authority under the bishop of Rome. The term *pope* was originally used broadly for priests and is related to the word *father*, but it eventually became an exclusive term to describe the Roman bishop in the West. In the modern sense of the word, it might be more accurate to refer to "the bishop of Rome" before the year 440, and to "the pope" after that.

The initial power of the Roman bishop seems to have been rooted in the civil structure of Rome and the prestige of his home, but there was clearly nothing like absolute authority for the first few centuries. Consider that the Council of Constantinople convened without the bishop of Rome's involvement! But just fifty years later, Cyril would write a letter to Pope Celestine I, asking for guidance in dealing with Nestorius, the archbishop of Constantinople.

But Roman authority was still a work in progress. After all, Celestine condemned Nestorianism before the Council of Ephesus reopened discussion on the issue. Clearly, they did not assume his word was final. As the capital of the old empire, Rome had a great deal of prestige and influence, but despite later claims made by Roman Catholicism, there is no evidence of *authority* during the first three centuries of Christianity.

Damasus (bishop of Rome from 366 to 384) was the first to explicitly claim special authority for Rome on the basis of apostolic succession: "Although the East sent the apostles, yet because of the merit of their martyrdom, Rome has acquired a superior right to claim them as citizens."[17] Damasus's successor, Siricius (384–399), was the first to apply the phrase "the burden of all the churches" (see 2 Corinthians 11:28) to the ministry of the popes, but this seems to have been theoretical rather than practical until the papacy of Leo the Great (440–461).[18] Leo was not an impressive theologian, but he was a skilled leader and negotiator.

Evangelism and Expansion

The most obvious source of conversion during this period, for better or for worse, was the Christianization of the Roman Empire. Becoming a disciple of Christ was no longer a cross to bear; it was eventually a legal mandate inseparable from Roman citizenship. Still, two missionaries are especially important from this period for their work in taking Christianity beyond the boundaries of the Roman Empire.

One was Ulfilas (311–383). As a young man, he was sent to Constantinople to study under the Arian theologian Lucian of Antioch. It was during this time that Ulfilas was consecrated bishop of the Goths (Germanic tribes from central Asia) and charged with the mission of bringing the Good News to these people. He is especially important because of his work on the creation of the Gothic alphabet to facilitate the translation of the Bible into the common tongue of the people. Though no Gothic manuscripts have survived, later writings preserved portions of them.

The second missionary, Patrick (ca. 415–493), was born to wealthy parents in Roman Britain. At the age of sixteen, he was abducted by Irish raiders and taken to Ireland as a slave. He eventually escaped and made his way back to his family, but he felt called to return to Ireland and evangelize the people there. Patrick is credited with converting thousands of pagans to Christianity, and he is honored throughout the world. Legend remembers him for his use of the shamrock to explain the doctrine of the Trinity and for driving the snakes from Ireland, but the true strength of his legacy is as a humble servant of Christ. In his Confession, he writes:

> Wherefore then, even if I should wish to part with them, and thus proceeding to Britain—and glad and ready I was to do so—as to my fatherland and kindred, and not that only, but to go as far as Gaul in order to visit the brethren and to behold the face of the saints of my Lord—God knoweth that I used to desire it exceedingly—yet *I am bound in the Spirit*, who *witnesseth to me* that if I should do this, he would note me as guilty; and I fear to lose the labour which I began; and yet not I, but Christ the Lord who commanded me to come and be with them for the remainder of my life, if the Lord will, and if he should keep me from every evil way, so that I may not sin in his sight.[19]

Boundaries of the Community

The earliest explicit reference to infant baptism is in Tertullian's *Concerning Baptism* (ca. 200), where he argues against the practice. Infant baptism is an ancient practice, but even in the time of Constantine, the normal pattern was to baptize those who had personally converted.[20] But as being Roman and being Christian became synonymous, infant baptism became increasingly common and a natural analogy to circumcision. For those outside the empire, baptism came after conversion, and with it membership in the community. On the opposite side, the boundaries by which someone was excluded from the community were expanded. One of the innovations of Nicaea was placing anathemas (curses) on those who rejected the declarations of the council. Previously, anathemas had been used occasionally, but never before with creeds that went beyond the language of Scripture. Those who wished to remain in the community had to have a proper understanding of Jesus as fully human and fully divine, with two natures in one person.

Discipleship

Two developments in discipleship during this period are especially noteworthy. First, Jerome's translation of the Bible into the Latin Vulgate made it accessible to the Western church. Though, in future generations, the practice of holding worship services in Latin would prevent the average Catholic from understanding what was taught, at this time Latin was the main language of the empire. It took some time for the standardized Vulgate to replace the older Latin versions, but once it did, its influence remained unmatched. The major English translations up through the King James Version are heavily influenced by Jerome's work, and even today the standard Roman Catholic translation is an updated Vulgate.

Second was the development of the monastery. In the East, Basil of Caesarea (329–379), often called Basil the Great, was a leading figure in the debate against the Arians. The elder brother of Gregory of Nyssa (an important theologian in his own right), Basil resolved to reject the world completely and live in seclusion, focusing on prayer and self-denial. But he decided that life in a separated community of like-minded believers was better than total isolation. He was not the first Christian to experiment with monasticism, but it was still a novelty at this point, and his influence was formative in transferring the movement from individuals to communities of thirty or forty monks.

While in previous generations, popular piety imagined martyrs as a higher class of believers, the monastic movement opened another way of sacrifice—the "white martyrdom" of self-denial. In Basil's case, his ascetic lifestyle combined with his prior bad health probably contributed to his early death. Basil taught the importance of hard physical labor alongside frequent organized worship, and allowed his monks only one meal a day (consisting of bread, water, and herbs), but he lived in the same conditions himself, sleeping on the ground and owning only one set of clothes. Compared to the isolated monks before him, this was quite lenient. Basil's monasticism was not one of pure hermitage, however: He frequently left the monastery on missionary journeys and preached, his monks were involved in social relief work, and the monasteries were connected to the local bishop. In many ways, Basil set the shape of community monasticism that has continued to this day.

7

The Early Middle Ages

(AD 476–AD 1000)

AFTER THE DEATH OF THEODOSIUS IN 395, when the empire was split between his two sons, Arcadius and Honorius, Rome was never again ruled by a single emperor. The Western, Latin-speaking empire fell in 410 when the Visigoths sacked Rome, but it took another sixty-six years to finally die. Internal political disputes, external enemies who smelled blood in the water, and the sheer financial burden of the empire all contributed to the demise. During the last twenty-one years, there were nine rulers, six of whom lasted less than three years. The final Western emperor, Romulus Augustus, was deposed in September of 476, taking with him the title of Augustus that had launched the Roman Empire.

The sacking of the city of Rome and the eventual collapse of the empire sent shock waves throughout the ancient world. What had seemed to be steady and secure was now overrun. Was it a judgment for forsaking the old Roman gods? What kind of future could there be—beyond nihilism and despair—with the unity of the known world broken? Augustine's *City of God*, written in response to the fall of Rome, emphasizes God's continuing sovereignty. Augustine's efforts to answer the questions of a society overwhelmed by insecurity might explain much of his emphasis on predestination and God's overruling providence.

The Eastern empire (often called the Byzantine Empire for the sake of clarity, though that title wasn't used until the reign of Justinian in about 527) survived and even prospered at times. Theodosius II, the same emperor who convened the Council of Constantinople, formalized the legal code and successfully bribed the army of Attila the Hun in exchange for peace.

Theodosius's successor, Marcian, convened the fourth ecumenical council, the Council of Chalcedon, in 451, but faced attacks from the Vandals. Like the Visigoths, the Vandals were Arians, but their invasion was partially motivated by theology. They believed they were the true church. When they drove out the leaders of Carthage and took over in 439, the office of bishop went unfilled for almost twenty-five years. The church there never fully recovered, which partially explains its vulnerability at the time of the Islamic ascendancy.

Most prominent among the Byzantine emperors was Justinian (482–565), who named his wife, Theodora, as his co-regent. Justinian revised and modernized the legal code, building on the work of Theodosius, and was able to recapture North Africa from the Vandals. In 535, he attempted to defeat the Ostrogoths in Italy, but after early successes became embroiled in the conflict for eighteen years. He finally regained control of Italy, but at great cost.

Meanwhile, theological divisions continued to roil the empire. The Montanists continued to call the church to reform, and

Justinian deliberately pursued them, effectively eliminating the movement (though some remnants survived until at least the ninth century). Many Monophysites also remained (including Theodora), prompting Justinian to seek some sort of compromise to appease them.

He called on Pope Vigilius to condemn some of the writers who favored Nestorianism, so that the Monophysites might be won over by his devotion to persecuting a common enemy. But the pope was uneasy. He condemned Menas (the bishop of Constantinople) and some of the emperor's supporters in 547 and then withdrew his censure.

In 551, after Justinian issued a decree against those he considered to have Nestorian sympathies, the pope once again issued an anathema against Menas, and again withdrew it. To resolve the issue, Justinian convened the Second Council of Constantinople (553). Once again, the vast majority of the bishops in attendance were Eastern, and in protest the pope did not attend. The council condemned several earlier theologians, including Origen (though there is some dispute about that), and the aftermath of the convocation was fraught with drama. Pope Vigilius was briefly exiled, some temporary schisms were created, and no progress was made with the Monophysites. Eventually, Vigilius accepted the council and revoked his previous support for the condemned writers. Power struggles between the emperor in the East and the pope in the West continued, and these would only intensify with later controversies.

The Monastic Movement

Early in the history of Christianity, monasticism was a highly individualized experience. People went off alone, focused on self-denial, and lived in isolation. As we saw in the previous chapter,

Basil successfully transitioned much of that disorganized asceticism into organized monasteries, for both service and worship. Benedict of Nursia (480–550) played a similar role in the West. Frustrated with the spiritual complacency that imperial favor had brought to Rome, he left to live in a cave in about the year 500. Others were drawn to him, a crowd gathered, and he began organizing monasteries. His most famous legacy is *The Rule of Benedict* (540), a practical handbook to guide the lives of monks. It includes a central focus on Scripture, and it became the dominant form of monasticism in the West through the end of the first millennium. The monks became expert scribes, copying books and preserving many that otherwise would have been lost.

Irish monasticism developed parallel to both Eastern and Western movements, and there, too, was an emphasis on learning. One monk, Columban (521–597), apparently triggered a war over a book, and tradition claims that he looked at the three thousand dead and decided to make up for it with three thousand converts. To that end, he started a community in Iona in 563 that became the center of Celtic Christianity. Although the Celtic monastic movement was essentially replaced by the Benedictine model within a century, the evangelistic successes remained.

Shifting Power: The Rising Papacy and the Holy Roman Empire

Gregory the Great (540–604) was born the son of a senator, but he sold his property, gave the money to the poor, and founded seven monasteries before joining one himself in about 574. After a few years in the monastery, Gregory was compelled by the pope to take a high-ranking position in the Imperial Court in 578; but in 585 he successfully returned to the monastery. In 590, despite his protests, he became pope. By this point, the papacy was a lavish and extravagant office, more like that of the pagan kings than the sacrificial mission work of the apostles.

Gregory was the first monk elected pope, and he returned the papacy to its religious mission. He negotiated treaties, sent missionaries, reformed the church's administration, codified church law, and helped the poor. He even worked with the Lombards in Italy, who were a constant threat to Rome. Gregory is one of the most important figures in cementing the papal power in the power vacuum caused after the fall of the Western empire. Interestingly, though Gregory personally refused the title of pope, it is plain that he was the effective founder of the modern office.

It is useful to consider the evidence that, even at this point, when the pope was clearly supreme among those still in communion with the mainstream church, he was not considered beyond challenge. The entire purpose of the fifth ecumenical council was to deal with a conflict between the pope and the emperor, and when the bishops sided with Justinian, the pope ultimately accepted their decision.

Another important example is Pope Honorius I (628–639). Monothelites, who claimed Christ only had one will and were therefore rebranded as Monophysites, were causing controversy in the church, and certain leaders wrote to Honorius asking for help. He responded so clearly in support of the Monothelite position that in the sixth ecumenical council, he was declared anathema, and it was signed by every delegate, including the emperor and the representatives of Pope Leo II. Today, apologists for the doctrine of papal infallibility tend to argue that this was not formal teaching. But the letter wasn't private; it was a formal reply to an officially submitted question.

Papal power did not remain merely religious, however. In 751, Pope Zachary used his influence to secure the power of Pepin the

Short (or Pepin III) over the Franks. When Pepin later conquered some territory in Italy, the Byzantine emperor (Constantine V) thanked him for his service and asked for the territory back. In a move apparently born both of political shrewdness and religious sincerity, Pepin declined and donated it to the pope instead in 754. This land became the core of the papal states, where the church no longer operated as a private landowner but as a separate sovereign political entity. With Pepin's death in 768, this transition had only just begun.

Though Pepin was an effective and wise ruler, one of his sons has far overshadowed him in history. Charles the Great, known as Charlemagne, ruled well, particularly after his brother's death in 771, and within a few decades, he had successfully conquered almost all of Christian Europe.

In 800, when Charlemagne went to Saint Peter's Basilica in Rome to celebrate Christmas, he was crowned emperor by Pope Leo III. Charlemagne was apparently surprised by this and never claimed authority over the East. Though the term *Holy Roman Empire* did not come into use for several more centuries, it is used to distinguish the territory ruled by Charlemagne from the earlier Roman Empire and the Byzantine Empire in the East. Charlemagne's successors controlled steadily less territory, as wars and infighting broke the united hegemony apart; after the initial period, the Holy Roman Empire is best understood as a name for Germany. The title of Holy Roman Emperor was not used between 924 and 962, when the German Otto I, already king of Italy, was crowned emperor by Pope John XII. As secular power increasingly depended on the pope's favor, the papacy continued to accumulate influence and authority. The lack of strong secular leaders as rivals meant that in the West, the emperor's power was eroded, even when he maintained or expanded his territory.

Birth of Islam

With the effective eradication of Roman paganism, Christianity had no serious religious competitors outside of its own sects. This changed with the arrival of Mohammed (570–632), who claimed to receive revelations from the angel Gabriel that he eventually wrote in the Quran. Initially, Mohammed met serious opposition and fled from Mecca to Medina, which remain two of the holiest sites in Islam. By 630, his troops had conquered a large portion of the Arabian Peninsula, including Mecca. His death shortly thereafter did not slow the expansion, though a dispute over his successor, or caliph, split the faith into two branches of Islam: Sunni and Shia. The Mohammedan armies believed in spreading the faith through holy war (jihad), and did so with extraordinary effectiveness. They conquered Palestine, northern Africa, and Spain, and were only stopped at the Battle of Tours in 732.

Islam emphasizes the oneness of God, treating Jesus as a prophet. Muslims believe that the suffering of Jesus on the cross was only apparent and not actual (Docetism). Just as Christianity was able to reform the disorganized paganism of Rome, Islam took the nomadic tribes of Arabia and gave them unity and real power for the first time in centuries. Though the map of the ancient world was redrawn dramatically and quickly, it did not immediately change life on the ground as dramatically as one might expect. Christians were still able to travel to Palestine to worship at the traditional places considered milestones in Jesus' life, and they did not face substantial persecution until after the turn of the millennium.

Icons

For the time being, the greatest religious conflict was not between Islam and Christianity, but between Eastern Christianity and

Western Christianity. The flash point was the use of icons: paintings of Christ or the saints, displayed in the churches as aids to worship. Icons had been periodically attacked at various times, but it was the rise of Islam that brought the issue to a head. When Muslims saw the icons, they accused the Christians of idolatry. Church leaders had always been careful to explain that the icons were representations that should not be worshiped, but in popular piety they became like magical talismans, powerful for their own sake.

Emperor Leo summoned a council and issued a ban on icons in churches in 726. Those who plastered over church murals and destroyed paintings were called iconoclasts—image breakers. Among the elites, iconoclasm was seen as a reasonable response to the excesses of the people and the defense against Islam. To the common people, including broad swaths of local clergy, it was unacceptable. Soldiers carrying out the edict were attacked by mobs, and the patriarch of Constantinople rebelled in 730. The emperor deposed him. Pope Gregory II anathematized the iconoclasts, rejecting their council as illegitimate. Tensions between East and West, brewing for centuries and now without the glue of a common empire to unite them, drastically increased.

Leo was not particularly aggressive about enforcing the edict in the face of all the opposition, but his son Constantine V (741–775) was committed to the cause. He convened another council and emphasized that the only proper representation of Christ was in the Communion bread. He shut down many monasteries, executed the patriarch of Constantinople, and tortured and killed many others. This persecution continued until Constantine and his immediate successor, Leo IV, died.

Leo's successor was his ten-year-old son, Constantine VI. Consequently, Leo's widow, Empress Irene, wielded power for most of her son's reign. She stopped the destruction of icons, allowed the monasteries to reopen, and convened the seventh (and final) true ecumenical council: the Second Council of Nicaea (787). According to this council, the veneration of icons that stopped short of worship was reaffirmed. Still, the controversy continued, and it wasn't until centuries later that the Western church accepted the second Nicaean council as ecumenical. Ultimately, the use of icons was accepted in both the East and West. Nevertheless, the division between the two halves of Christendom continued to deepen, and the behavior of the Byzantine emperor tightened the relationship between the Western churches and the Holy Roman Empire, exacerbating the divide.

Evangelism and Expansion

During this period, the gospel continued to spread. Ethelbert of Kent, the first Anglo-Saxon king to convert to Christianity, was baptized in 597 by Augustine of Canterbury (not to be confused with the long-dead Augustine of Hippo). Just over a century later, in 716, Boniface traveled to Germany and pioneered the Christianization of the Germanic people. Though there were pockets of Christianity in Ireland and Scotland prior to this time, it was also during this period that missionaries such as Columba and Aidan helped to spread Christianity throughout these areas of the British Isles.

Cyril and Methodius were missionaries who traveled to the Slavs in 862, helping to spread Christianity throughout the Slavic region. In 988, Prince Vladimir of Kiev was baptized, leading to the mass conversion of the people of Kiev. This is considered the beginning of the Christianization of Russia, where the Russian Orthodox Church continues to hold considerable sway even today.

Boundaries of the Community

By this point, the entrance to the church was well established. But what were the outer boundaries of the community? One element of discipleship forces us to face the reality that we do not always live up to the pattern of Christ. What do we do after we sin? Initially, penance was created to deal with those who had abandoned the faith under the great persecution, and the concept was expanded until it referred to public confession of serious sin. In the Celtic church, penance became a way to deal with any sin. Sin could be confessed privately to a priest, who would provide some assignment in response. Eventually, lists were created called *penitentials*, providing suggested penances for various sins. When these were taken to Rome, they became the basis of the modern Roman Catholic practice of confession.

Even today, Christians disagree on where the balance should be struck between two apparently contradictory mandates in the New Testament. On the one hand, no one is perfect in this life, and the church is inevitably a hospital for sinners (1 John 1:8). Paul tells us in Galatians 6:1, "If another believer is overcome by some sin, you who are godly should gently and humbly help that person back onto the right path. And be careful not to fall into the same temptation yourself." On the other hand, Christians are called to "be holy because [God is] holy" (1 Peter 1:16), and Paul tells us we should not even eat "with anyone who claims to be a believer yet indulges in sexual sin, or is greedy, or worships idols, or is abusive, or is a drunkard, or cheats people" (1 Corinthians 5:11). It is the church's responsibility to be both loving and righteous.

Discipleship

Michael Green argues persuasively that the temptation to ritualism that seems so excessive in the Middle Ages was actually seeded by the heresies addressed in the New Testament.[1] We'll always be tempted to look for the visible and the tangible instead of those things that can only be perceived by faith. To many evangelicals, the use of icons is a clear example of the human temptation to succumb to idolatry in the same way the Israelites so often did. When Aaron fashioned the golden calf, he said: "O Israel, these are the gods [*Elohim*] who brought you out of the land of Egypt!" (Exodus 32:4). It seems that their sin was not in replacing YHWH, but in worshiping the invisible God through a statue. But where is the line now that Jesus has come in the flesh? The Second Council of Nicaea drew the line between veneration and worship.

8

The High Middle Ages

(AD 1000–AD 1300)

IN THE HEAT OF JUNE 1215, King John of England formally approved a document that would reshape the government of the nation and its eventual colonies. It provided certain rights to barons and other free men, and placed even the king himself under the authority of the law. Why would a sovereign king willingly agree to these terms? It may have had something to do with the army his barons had assembled at Runnymede, and their refusal to swear allegiance to the king until their demands were met. Facing a stalemate, the king and the barons turned to another authority—the pope—to settle their dispute.

Pope Innocent III (1160–1216) was a cunning leader who knew the extent of his power and was willing to employ it whenever necessary. As the influence of the papacy grew, national leaders began to treat the pope as the supreme ruler. He had the authority to excommunicate national leaders, cutting them off from the life of the church, and he could place entire nations under interdiction, putting a stop to public worship and all sacraments except baptism and last rites. This kind of pressure could break a ruler, and as the influence of the papacy grew, national leaders began to treat the pope as a supreme leader.

When John attempted to overrule the appointment of the Archbishop of Canterbury, the pope placed England under an interdict and excommunicated the king. Eventually, under pressure from the barons, John agreed to submit to the pope's rule—paying an annual tribute to Rome and making England a vassal of the pope. John was restored in 1213, and the barons were temporarily appeased.

But by 1215, the barons were ascendant again. With their first set of demands, John appealed to Pope Innocent for aid. When the pope sided with his vassal, the barons gathered a rebellious army. At the tip of the sword, King John agreed to sign what became the Magna Carta—though he never intended to keep the terms of the agreement. When he wrote to the pope asking for the charter to be annulled, Innocent obliged. Civil war would certainly have broken out had John not died on October 18, 1216. His nine-year-old son, Henry, was crowned, and his supporters approved the Magna Carta—now, remarkably, with the pope's approval.

The Magna Carta laid out the principle of the rule of law, a radical concept that shaped the future of Western society. This story demonstrates the complicated web of political and religious power during the High Middle Ages. The power vacuum from the fall of Rome had been filled in Europe, but the conflict between East and West, secular and religious rulers, and eventually Christianity and Islam remained.

Schisms and Controversies

The conflict between the Eastern and Western churches had continued to develop since the fall of the Roman Empire. One key dispute was over the addition of the *filioque* clause to the Nicene Creed by the Western church. The Nicene Creed, as approved at the Council of Constantinople, described the Holy Spirit as proceeding from the Father, but the Western church modified the wording to say that the Spirit proceeded from the Father *and* the Son. It is probably fair to say that the doctrinal issue is opaque to most Christians: What difference does it make? The implications for our understanding of the Trinity are subtle, though not unimportant. But the real conflict is much clearer. Eastern churches were offended that the Western church felt qualified to change an ecumenical creed without council or consultation. The authority of the pope had gradually been developing, but this crossed a line.

In 861, Photius, the patriarch of Constantinople, was deposed and exiled for opposing the emperor, who favored a union of the Eastern and Western churches. In 867, Photius was restored as patriarch, but in 869–870 the Third Council of Constantinople (also called the Eighth Ecumenical Council) anathematized him and reaffirmed the decision of an earlier council that the bishop of Rome held primacy among all bishops. The Great Schism became formal in 1054. Pope Leo IX excommunicated the bishop of Constantinople, Patriarch Michael I. Michael responded by excommunicating Leo. The two churches remain divided to this day.

Defining the power of religious and secular rulers remained controversial. Should the secular authorities have power over the religious realm? Or should the religious powers control the state? This issue may seem strange to those living in the liberal West, but from the time of Constantine on, nations had been Christianized when their leaders were Christianized. It was reasonable to wonder what sort of hierarchy this created. The Investiture Controversy, a dispute about who had the right to appoint bishops and abbots, was a major issue between the papacy and various European monarchs throughout this period. It was finally resolved in 1122 by the Concordat of Worms, which gave the church the power to appoint its own bishops but allowed secular rulers to participate in confirming them.

The Fourth Lateran Council (1215) was one of the most important events of the High Middle Ages. Convened by Pope Innocent III, it approved a number of new doctrines and regulations, including the requirement that all Catholics receive the Eucharist at least once a year, and that priests hear confession from their parishioners at least once a year. It also confirmed the doctrine of transubstantiation, which holds that the bread and wine of Communion are transformed into the body and blood of Christ when blessed by the priest. It is difficult to trace the development of this doctrine because the earliest references to Communion follow the language of the New Testament very closely. It is hard to say whether "this is Christ's body" means transubstantiation when the entire debate is over what "this is my body" means. Perhaps most significantly, the council also approved the use of force in certain cases to combat heresy, laying the groundwork for the Inquisition.

The Waldensian Movement

One fascinating controversy was over the Waldensians. In 1989, *Christian History* magazine ran an issue titled, "Waldensians: Medieval 'Evangelicals.'"[1] They take their name from Peter Waldo, a wealthy merchant who commissioned the translation of several books of the Bible into his local dialect and took the words of

Mark 10:21 literally: "Go and sell all your possessions and give the money to the poor, and you will have treasure in heaven. Then come, follow me." His followers also embraced poverty, and both men and women went out in the streets, preaching and calling people to repentance. Their doctrine seems more at home in 1720 than 1120, the date assigned to this statement of faith:

> **Article VIII**: In like manner, we firmly hold, that there is no other mediator and advocate with God the Father, save only Jesus Christ. And as for the Virgin Mary, that she was holy, humble, and full of grace; and in like manner do we believe concerning all the other saints, viz: that being in heaven, they wait for the resurrection of their bodies at the day of judgment.
>
> **Article IX**: *Item*, we believe that after this life, there are only two places, the one for the saved, and the other for the damned, the which two places we call paradise and hell, absolutely denying that purgatory invented by antichrist, and forged contrary to the truth.
>
> **Article X**: *Item*, we have always accounted as an unspeakable abomination before God, all those inventions of men, namely, the feasts and the vigils of saints, the water which they call holy. As likewise to abstain from flesh upon certain days, and the like; but especially their masses.
>
> **Article XI**: We esteem for an abomination and as antichristian, all those human inventions which are a trouble or prejudice to the liberty of the spirit.
>
> **Article XII**: We do believe that the sacraments are signs of the holy thing, or visible forms of the invisible grace, accounting it good that the faithful sometimes use the

said signs or visible forms, if it may be done. However, we believe and hold, that the above said faithful may be saved without receiving the signs aforesaid, in case they have no place nor any means to use them.

Article XIII: We acknowledge no other sacrament but Baptism and the Lord's Supper.[2]

The Waldensians, also known as Waldenses, were condemned by the Council of Verona in 1184 and the Fourth Lateran Council in 1215, but they persisted despite persecution and massacres. Most of their documents were destroyed in a purge in 1559, and thus many of our sources are written from the perspectives of their adversaries (a recurring problem when evaluating groups condemned as heretical).

The Waldenses claimed their convictions predated Waldo, tracing back to the time of the apostles. Though there is not much evidence to support this,[3] it does show that they were concerned with refuting the idea that their doctrines were corruptions of the faith preserved in the mainstream Church.[4]

The most important point in our consideration of this movement is that the Reformation did not spring from the mind of Martin Luther out of nothing; throughout Christian history, there were reformers who challenged the doctrine and holiness of their brothers and sisters. Condemned for unauthorized preaching (even Waldo remained a layman), the Waldenses were later falsely accused of Manichaeanism (a dualistic Gnostic religious movement dating to third-century Persia) and suffered persecution until being mostly absorbed in the Protestant Reformation.

The Crusades

There are few Christians who would consider the Crusades a bright spot in history. Often, they were counterproductive to the cause of genuine conversion, motivated more by politics than piety, and excessively cruel. However, it would be a mistake to neglect the fact that Islam was a very real threat during the Middle Ages. The Muslim armies had been stopped at the Battle of Tours in 732, but in the eleventh century, the Seljuks (an ascendant extremist group) captured Baghdad and would no longer allow Christian pilgrims access to Palestine.

In 1071, the Seljuks began advancing against the Byzantine Empire, conquering Antioch and even Nice by 1085. The threat of Muslim advancement, reaction to the treatment of Christian pilgrims, and a sense of outrage at the abuse of holy sites all contributed to the Crusades, but there were other, more mundane reasons as well. For great masses of peasants and low-level nobles alike, the Crusades offered a way to seek a better future. For the church, they provided a way to unify Christendom around a common cause. These motivations were not secret, and when Pope Urban II called for the First Crusade in 1095, he made them quite explicit:

> This land which you inhabit . . . is too narrow for your
> large population; nor does it abound in wealth; and it
> furnishes scarcely food enough for its cultivators. Hence
> it is that you murder and devour one another . . . enter
> upon the road to the Holy Sepulchre; wrest that land
> from the wicked race, and subject it to yourselves.[5]

It is too simplistic to see the Crusades as either purely selfish or purely religious. Like most human actions, they were motivated by a mixture of desires. Though there were seven major Crusades, the actual effects in Palestine were minor. The First Crusade was poorly organized, and the first wave was made up primarily of common people rather than soldiers; still, it was the most successful. In 1099,

Crusaders took Jerusalem and established the Latin kingdom of Jerusalem, which persisted until 1291. The most bizarre Crusade was the fourth (1202), which was supposed to go to Jerusalem. But the knights couldn't pay the fees the Venetians required for transport. They agreed to a trade: passage to Jerusalem in exchange for the Crusaders first sacking a small Christian town and then Constantinople. Apparently, the Crusaders vented their bloodlust in the earlier battles and lost all interest in going to Jerusalem. Constantinople never fully recovered, and the conflict did not ease the divisions between East and West. When the Seventh Crusade ended in 1254, Palestine was almost unchanged, Christendom was not reunited, most people were still poor, and papal power was in decline from its peak under Innocent III (1198–1216).

Although the outcome of the Crusades was basically failure, there were some important results. First, two centuries of warfare were costly in both lives and treasure. To spur recruitment, the pope offered a total remission of sins, called an indulgence, for Crusaders. Eventually, this offer was extended to those who contributed to the cause financially, and the sale of indulgences turned out to be one of the major points of conflict spurring the Protestant Reformation. These funds, raised ostensibly for the Crusades, brought in the revenue necessary for building the famous cathedrals of the era. Second, the papacy assimilated power during the Crusades as the leader of Christendom, but also lost much of this influence through a series of failures. Finally, and most positively, the new interaction with the Islamic world connected the West with learning that had been lost for centuries. The science and philosophy of the ancient Greeks, engaged by the apologists, had been forgotten in Western Christendom, but these schools of thought were still debated and developed among the Muslims. These rediscovered ideas laid the groundwork for the Scholastic movement.

Theological Bright Spots

Unfortunately, the bulk of our discussion in this chapter has been consumed with the negative developments of this era, which might leave you wondering why it could be called the High Middle Ages. The division of the Roman Catholic and Eastern Orthodox churches, violent elimination of disfavored sects, and confusion between conquest and evangelism of the Crusades do not sound like a promising start. But there was also a renaissance of learning at the same time. Scholastic philosophers, rediscovering the works of Aristotle, began to develop sophisticated theological systems. The supreme example of this was Thomas Aquinas (1225–1274), best known for his *Summa Theologica*, a massive set of questions and answers about doctrine.

This intellectual development is also apparent in the rise of the university system. Both the University of Paris (founded ca. 1045) and the University of Oxford (founded ca. 1096) served as important centers of religious training, building naturally on the intellectual pedigree of the earlier monastery system, which had emphasized learning from its inception. The monastic system continued to develop as well: Bernard joined the Cistercian order and founded the famous monastery at Clairvaux; Francis of Assisi renounced his wealth to follow the calling of God; and Dominic de Guzmán founded the Dominican order. These monks called for reform from within the institutional church and provided important challenges to the superstition and excesses of the early Middle Ages.

Evangelism and Expansion

The primary means of expansion during this period was through the Crusades. Temporarily, the Middle East was brought into Christendom, though in the constant give-and-take of war, the gains were not sustained. The lack of missionary activity during this period may have been because there were few places to take the gospel without the sword, and the priority for warfare was in the Middle East.

Boundaries of the Community

What did it mean to become a Christian in the age of the Crusades? Vanquished people were baptized in groups when their territory was conquered. This certainly led to impressive numbers, but the fruit of this approach should probably concern us. Compared to earlier generations when being a Christian was a decision made at personal cost, the spiritual health of the church was poor during this time. Centuries earlier, Charlemagne had required any parents who would not have their children baptized to be put to death, so the idea of forced conversion wasn't totally new, but it contributed to the fusion of national and religious identities.

Discipleship

Anselm (1033–1109), a theologian we haven't yet discussed, was extremely important to the discipleship of believers in the High Middle Ages. He has been called the Augustine of the Middle Ages. His best-known work was on the theory of atonement: What does it mean that Jesus died for our sins? Anselm articulated the "satisfaction theory" of atonement—that God, not Satan, was the one who was paid in the death of Christ. Many earlier theologians held to the "ransom theory" of atonement—that human beings are Satan's prisoners, but Christ's death paid the ransom to Satan for our release. Anselm argued that human beings deserve a penalty for our sins, a debt owed to God. Instead of demanding the impossible—that we repay God the honor and worship we have stolen from him—the infinite God became a man and died in our place, paying our debt to the Father. This refinement of the understanding of the death of Jesus helped prepare the way for the theories of Luther and Calvin in the Reformation.

9

The Late Middle Ages

(AD 1300–AD 1500)

In August 1519, Ulrich Zwingli, a Swiss clergyman, was away from home when he learned that the Black Death had broken out in the city of Zurich. He quickly returned to minister to the plague victims, but soon became infected himself. Though ravaged with the disease, he wrote his "Plague Hymn" at a time when it appeared unlikely he would recover:

> Help me, O Lord,
> My strength and rock;
> Lo, at the door
> I hear death's knock . . .
>
> My pains increase;
> Haste to console;

For fear and woe
Seize body and soul.

Death is at hand.
My senses fail.
My tongue is dumb;
Now, Christ, prevail.

Lo! Satan strains
To snatch his prey;
I feel his grasp;
Must I give way?

He harms me not,
I fear no loss,
For here I lie
Beneath thy cross.[1]

Though Zwingli recovered and wrote four more stanzas of his hymn praising God for his deliverance, countless others did not survive the plague. In the main outbreak a century and a half earlier (1347–1351), one-third to one-half the population of affected areas died.[2] Between plague, famine, and war, the world was in a period of turmoil that once again redrew boundaries on the world map and transformed the way Christians carried out the Great Commission.

John Wycliffe

It takes courage to stand up to the powerful and influential under the best of circumstances, and John Wycliffe (1330–1384) did not find himself in the best of circumstances. The church he saw was wealthy and indulgent, and he called it to reform. He came to reject the doctrines of transubstantiation and indulgences, and he emphasized justification by faith. Believing that these truths were clear from the Bible, he thought others would realize that as well if they could simply read the Scriptures for themselves. He decided to translate the Bible into English. The pope issued edicts against him, but Wycliffe died before he could be formally convicted of heresy. His translation was completed by John Purvey, but Wycliffe became known as "the morning star of the Reformation" for his work.[3] Though he did not live to see the full force of his efforts, and his followers were driven underground, the same arguments he had made would be picked up by the next generation.

The Weakening Papacy

The power of the papacy had steadily increased until the time of Pope Innocent III, but it gradually declined after that. During the late Middle Ages, this decay accelerated considerably, even as the Roman Church attempted to intensify claims of papal supremacy—through such means as the Unam Sanctam bull, a decree issued in 1302.

A major contributing factor to the weakening papacy was the so-called Papal Babylonian Captivity. During this period, from 1309 to 1377, the papacy was exiled from Rome to Avignon, France. In Avignon, the popes were largely under the control of the French kings, and their ability to exercise authority was greatly diminished. The Captivity also damaged the papacy's reputation, as many people began to question why the popes had allowed themselves to be exiled in the first place.

In the aftermath of Avignon, when Pope Gregory XI moved the papacy back to Rome, there arose a controversy called the

Second Great Schism, or Western Schism, which saw two (or sometimes three) men concurrently claiming to be the rightful pope. The schism weakened not only the papacy's practical efficiency but also its reputation; it is hard to claim that the pope is the clearly acknowledged head of all Christendom when you cannot agree on who the pope is. The Great Schism was not effectively resolved until the Council of Constance (1414–1418), during which three papal contenders resigned and a new pope was chosen. The Council of Constance is perhaps best known for condemning John Wycliffe and ordering the exhumation of his bones. Jan Hus, a Bohemian supporter of Wycliffe, was promised "safe conduct" to come to the council, but once he entered the city of Constance, he was arrested, tried on what seemed to be manufactured charges, and burned at the stake.

Dealing with "Heretics"

The execution of Hus and the humiliation of Wycliffe were not isolated incidents. Contemporaneous with the final Crusades was another effort to bring the Kingdom of God by the sword: the Inquisition. Gregory IX appointed the first inquisitors in 1232, and they were soon at work throughout Europe.

The Inquisition was responsible for the execution of many who were accused of being heretics, including members of the Knights Templar, an order that in previous generations had protected pilgrims during the Crusades. The Inquisition continued for hundreds of years, in three primary phases, taking the lives of thousands of people.

Several well-known individuals were also condemned during this intense period of heresy hunting, including some whose crimes do not seem particularly connected to Christian doctrine. Joan of Arc (1412–1431) was a young woman from a humble background who claimed she had received visions calling her to lead the French army against the English in the Hundred Years' War. Though not formally a commander, she led the troops successfully in several battles, but she was eventually captured by the English. They arranged for a religious trial (although her appeal to the pope was denied), and she was charged with seventy counts of heresy. The charges included claiming divine authority for prophecy, wearing men's clothing, and claiming assurance of salvation.

When Joan was sentenced to death, she recanted, and her punishment was commuted to life imprisonment. Three days later, when she was seen wearing men's clothes again, her original sentence was reinstated. The nineteen-year-old woman prayed for her enemies before being tied to the stake, and as the flames took her, her final word was "Jesus." Twenty-five years later, her family appealed her case to the pope, who annulled the judgment of the earlier court. On May 16, 1920, she was canonized as a saint.

These collisions of politics, pride, and faith are an important warning for Christians of all generations. Whenever human beings are involved, there is always the temptation to take things (both positive and negative) personally, or to raise our preferences and opinions to the level of doctrinal certainty. When the church acquires absolute power, there is always a risk of abusing it.

The Brave New World

One reason the church was so eager to hold on to power is that the world was rapidly changing. In addition to the huge number of deaths associated with the plague, important transitions were underway. The Byzantine Empire had gradually been fading in power and prestige since the sacking of Constantinople during the Fourth Crusade, and a continual onslaught of enemies had drained what little strength the nation empire had left. In 1453, the Turks destroyed Constantinople, and the formerly proud Eastern empire was completely conquered by 1460. The last vestiges of the true Roman Empire also fell after 1500 years, although the Germanic people continued to use the title of Holy Roman Empire.

In 1492, Christopher Columbus sailed across the Atlantic Ocean, intending to find a shortcut to Asia. Instead, he established a connection between the Americas and Europe that remains important to the present day. The migration to the so-called New World, including the sending of missionaries who would bring the gospel, belongs to the next era, but Columbus's voyage is another example of the transitions that were underway, reshaping people's understanding of what they knew and laying the groundwork for changes that would affect the church as well.

Another major breakthrough was the invention of the movable-type printing press. Prior to the time of Johannes Gutenberg (1400–1468), printing was an expensive, time-consuming, and skilled process that limited the publication of books. Gutenberg's press made it possible to produce volumes much more efficiently and affordably. His major project was the Gutenberg Bible, an edition of the Latin Vulgate. The early editions were still prohibitively expensive for individuals, but the technological revolution he began ultimately made the Bible accessible to the masses, who previously could never have dreamed of owning their own copy.

Evangelism and Expansion

During this period, there was little expansion of the church, except what was taken naturally to colonies. Islamic forces conquered substantial territory from the Eastern church, so that territory was actually *lost* in that region. God's Kingdom was not in retreat, however, and the process of marching forward to the uttermost parts of the earth would soon resume.

Boundaries of the Community

The boundaries of the community in this period were still marked by the same trends as earlier in the Middle Ages. Primarily, the difference was the work of the Inquisitors, who sought out perceived enemies of the church for punishment. The most famous example of this was the Spanish Inquisition, in which Ferdinand and Isabella tried to unite their kingdom by driving out Jews and Muslims. This effort persisted from the 1480s to the end of the century, and resumed again during the Protestant Reformation.

Discipleship

Discipleship was at a low ebb at the end of the Middle Ages. Reformers such as Wycliffe and Hus had limited influence over the populace, and the common people were steeped in ritualism that verged on magical thinking. One important exception within the Catholic church were the mystical reformers, including Catherine of Siena (1347–1380) and Thomas à Kempis (ca. 1380–1471). Catherine claimed to receive visions and called people to a higher, more intense form of worship. Thomas, a German monk, wrote *The Imitation of Christ*, a practical model for pursuing perfection in Christlikeness. The influence of his writing continues to our present day.

10

The Reformation Era

(AD 1500–AD 1700)

IT WOULD BE DIFFICULT TO EVALUATE this period of Christian history without discussing Galileo Galilei (1564–1642). Many of Galileo's predecessors worked from Aristotle's "four causes," which seek to determine *why* physical change occurs. Galileo instead worked on *how* change occurs, and from this laid the groundwork for Newtonian physics. His experimental approach led him to point his telescope at the stars, and his observations confirmed the theory of Copernicus that Earth revolves around the sun, rather than being fixed in space.

In 1615, Galileo wrote a lengthy letter reconciling Scripture with the idea that the earth moves, explaining that the biblical language that would seem to contradict a heliocentric view comes from God's accommodation to human understanding (such as in 1 Chronicles 16:30). Galileo's approach was condemned in 1616, and the idea that the earth is not the fixed center of the cosmos was condemned as heretical. Galileo agreed to stop teaching the theory and did so until 1623, when one of his friends became pope.

The election of Pope Urban VIII seemed to embolden Galileo, who felt he could once again discuss his ideas as long as he couched them in hypothetical language. Apparently he presumed too much, and the imagined dialogue he wrote in 1632 put the pope's favorite arguments into the mouth of a fool. Galileo was called before the Inquisition and threatened with torture (though he was never actually tortured), and eventually he recanted.

It is probably only an urban legend that he said, "*Eppur si muove*" ("Nevertheless, it moves") after agreeing to their charges, but the phrase does represent Galileo's apparently pragmatic attitude: "I will say what I need to say, but the truth is unchanged." Galileo spent the final decade of his life under house arrest, and he wasn't formally vindicated by the Catholic church until 1992.

Galileo's conflict with the pope is sometimes used in debates about the relationship of faith and science; but it really has more to do with the nature of authority. In *Christianity's Dangerous Idea*, theologian Alister McGrath summarizes the issue well:

> At its heart, the emergence and growth of Protestantism concerned one of the most fundamental questions that can confront any religion: Who has the authority to define its faith? Institutions or individuals? Who has the right to interpret its foundational document, the Bible?
>
> Protestantism took its stand on the right of individuals to interpret the Bible for themselves rather than be forced to submit to "official" interpretations handed down by popes or other centralized religious authorities. . . . [Martin] Luther's radical doctrine of

the "priesthood of all believers" empowered individual believers. It was a radical, dangerous idea that bypassed the idea that a centralized authority had the right to interpret the Bible. There was no centralized authority, no clerical monopoly on biblical interpretation. A radical reshaping of Christianity was inevitable, precisely because the restraints on change had suddenly—seemingly irreversibly—been removed.[1]

God's Word in Man's Tongue

The greatest and most important development during the Protestant Reformation was making the Bible available in the common language of the people. One of the men most responsible for making this possible was Desiderius Erasmus (1466–1536), one of the preeminent scholars of his age. At one point, one in every ten books sold in Europe bore the name of Erasmus, but because he attacked the corruption in the church without joining the Protestant Reformation, he ended up pleasing no one. Still, when he produced a modern edition of the Greek New Testament in 1516, with the goal that the Bible could be translated into every language, he provided the ore that would transform the world. One of the people most influenced by Erasmus's work was Martin Luther, who published a German edition of the New Testament in 1522.

Another key figure in early Bible translation was William Tyndale (1494–1536), and few could match his legacy. A brilliant priest who spoke seven languages, Tyndale could accomplish nearly anything he set his mind to. But his passion was not to build a name for himself or to engage in esoteric debates about advanced points of doctrine. Instead, he wanted to bring God's Word to God's people, so they could learn the good news of justification by faith. But when he asked his bishop for permission to translate the New Testament into English, and for money to support the project, he was denied. Tyndale went to Germany to complete his work (and even there he had to move from Cologne to Worms). In 1526, his New Testament was published and distributed in England, where it was quickly banned. Before he could finish the Old Testament, Tyndale was arrested. Tried for heresy, he was executed on October 6, 1536. Still, his translation formed the basis of the Coverdale Bible (1535), the Geneva Bible (1560), and the King James Version (1611).

After Tyndale's death, Miles Coverdale (1488–1569), who had worked with Tyndale on the Pentateuch, produced the Great Bible at the request of Thomas Cromwell, King Henry VIII's chief minister. The Great Bible was the first authorized English Bible produced. The accessibility of the Bible to the common people played no small part in the transformation of Western society.

Martin Luther and the Lutherans

Martin Luther (1483–1546) was a devoted monk. He focused on self-denial but lived in perpetual fear that his good works would never be enough to earn him a place in heaven. One day, while studying the book of Romans, he came to believe that the righteousness of God was not a standard one could attain, but rather a gift to be received by faith. This transformation worked its way through Luther's theology and ultimately throughout the world.

On October 31, 1517, Luther nailed a list of ninety-five theses— his "Disputation for Clarifying the Power of Indulgences"—to the door of the Castle Church in Wittenberg, Germany. It might be said that the church door was something like a community bulletin board, but that's misleading. Luther's theses were academic and written in Latin rather than German. They were intended not to persuade the public (though later, when translated into German, they had a widespread effect), but to initiate a scholarly dialogue among his fellow clerics. Their intended audience included Archbishop Albrecht of Mainz, whose sale of indulgences had prompted Luther to post the theses. Albrecht believed the theses were heretical, and by December 1517, formal heresy charges were being prepared against Luther.

Though much of the controversy is difficult for modern audiences to understand, a sampling of two theses reveals some of the areas of disagreement and captures Luther's rhetorical flair:

27. They "preach human opinions" who say that, as soon as a coin thrown into the money chest clinks, a soul flies out [of purgatory].

28. It is certain that when a coin clinks in the money chest profits and avarice may well be increased, but the intercession of the church rests on God's choice alone.[2]

This direct attack on a major source of church income did not sit well with Luther's superiors. By 1521, he had been called to stand before the Holy Roman Emperor, Charles V, at the Diet of Worms. Luther expected a debate but was given an ultimatum: Recant your views or be convicted of heresy.

Luther would not recant. Instead, he answered the most powerful people of his day: "Unless I am convicted by Scripture and plain reason—I do not accept the authority of popes and councils, for they have contradicted each other—my conscience is captive to the word of God. . . . Here I stand. I can do no other. God help me! Amen."[3]

Of the six electors present, two refused to sign the declaration condemning Luther as a heretic, but he was convicted by the majority. Because they had promised him safe passage, they intended to let him go home, and then arrest him and execute him later—better treatment than Jan Hus received! Luther's life was probably saved when he was kidnapped on the road home and taken to Wartburg Castle. Frederick the Wise (one of the two dissenting electors) had arranged for him to be captured and hidden, and Luther was thus able to work in secrecy at Wartburg for ten months. During that time, he wrote much, including translating the New Testament into German in just eleven weeks. The Protestant Reformation continued without his active presence, and soon spread beyond what he had imagined.

The word *Protestant* comes from the Latin *protestari*. In English, the word *protest* can have negative, reactionary connotations. By this understanding, Protestants are protesters because they turned their backs on the Roman church. But that is a misunderstanding. In Latin, *protestari* means "to testify" or "profess openly." Protestants take their name from the attitude of Luther's "here I stand," carrying on the legacy of Peter and John in Acts 4:20: "We cannot stop telling about everything we have seen and heard."

Certainly it would be an oversimplification to suggest that Luther produced a reform movement out of whole cloth and of his own accord. Instead, he was one of several people who arrived at similar convictions at the same time, building on the work of previous generations' discontentment with the state of the mainstream church.

So what was unique about 1517? Luther was a crucial player at a critical moment: The Word of God was becoming accessible to the common people, the Roman church's obvious corruption fueled criticism, and multiple claimants to the papacy had undermined confidence in the pope's absolute, infallible authority. People were ready to be called back to the Word of God. Perhaps even readier than Luther realized.

In his absence from Wittenberg, the leadership of the movement shifted to his fellow reformers Philipp Melanchthon and Andreas Karlstadt. On Christmas Day 1521, Karlstadt preached salvation by faith to two thousand in attendance, omitted from the traditional readings any reference to the Mass as a sacrifice, and gave instructions in German instead of Latin. Shortly thereafter, he called for the destruction of icons.

In response to the ensuing turmoil, Luther returned to Wittenberg in disguise. Were his enemies right? Was the doctrine of *sola scriptura* destined to produce only chaos and division? But there was no turning back now. The spark Luther had released was no longer under his control. Karlstadt subsequently left Wittenberg, dividing from Luther over how far they must go in leaving the traditions of Catholicism behind.

Charles V, the Holy Roman Emperor, soon realized that the issue would not be easily reversed. In 1526, he convened the Diet of Speyer, where it was determined that each territory's prince could choose to be either Catholic or Lutheran. If a Catholic lived in a Lutheran territory or vice versa, they could move somewhere more agreeable.

The emperor had little choice but to be flexible: The Muslim armies of Suleiman the Magnificent were demanding his full attention, and he was eventually able to drive them back. In 1547, after defeating the Turks a second time, and with Luther's death the year before, Charles took military action to defeat the Lutherans, whom he had only been tolerating until then. But although Charles won a military victory, the Lutherans were unwilling to return to Catholicism. In 1555, at the Diet of Augsburg, the principle that each territory could choose its own faith was reaffirmed, and Catholic and Lutheran doctrine were accorded equal status before the law.

But this was not quite freedom of religion! Anabaptists and Calvinists were still being executed as heretics. The 1530 Lutheran Augsburg Confession condemned older heretical groups such as the Arians, Manicheans, Novatians, and Pelagians, but Anabaptists were condemned five times by name and other times by implication.[4] Nevertheless, it was a start, and at the conclusion of the Thirty Years' War, the Peace of Westphalia (1648) expanded freedom to all religious minorities established before 1648. This proved impossible to enforce, and each territory could effectively choose its own religion. The Holy Roman Empire was impotent from this point forward, although the title remained until Napoleon abolished it in 1806.

Ulrich Zwingli

Born around the same time as Luther, Ulrich Zwingli (1484–1531) was an important leader in the Reformation in his own right. Although he was probably influenced by Luther's work, Zwingli rejected the title of Lutheran and emphasized that he had learned his doctrine from the New Testament, not from any human being. For our purposes, Zwingli is most important for his understanding of the church, baptism, and Communion.

Like Luther, Zwingli believed in the importance of a regional, visible church, unified by a common faith. In his mind, the people of Zurich were a new Jerusalem, united by their common Christianity and ruled by their civil leaders. He considered God's elect to include all citizens of Zurich ("save for a few Catholics").[5] With this philosophy, infant baptism made sense for the same reasons it had during the Roman Empire: Being a citizen and being a Christian were effectively the same. This stance also made it appropriate for civil authorities to enforce Christian doctrine and punish heretics. In the case of baptism, this became particularly important.

Some of Zwingli's followers believed he didn't go far enough in his reforms. A group of his friends and disciples were rejected by the city council for being too radical, and were given the choice to leave Zurich or face imprisonment. A few days later, one of them, George Blaurock, "asked Conrad Grebel, for the sake of God's will, to baptize him with a true Christian baptism on his own faith and confession."[6] He was baptized, despite the January chill, and then the rest of the group followed his example. For this, they were called Anabaptists (rebaptizers), although they denied rebaptizing anyone, and claimed that they were simply properly baptizing for the first time (a controversy that goes back at least as far as the Donatists).

One of the key leaders of the Anabaptists, Felix Manz, had been a disciple and personal friend of Zwingli's, but when he refused to recant, Zwingli showed no mercy. Manz's hands and feet were tied, and he was taken by boat out into the river. As he was thrown over the side to drown, his final words were, "Into thy hands, O Lord, I commend my spirit."[7]

As his old friend perished, Zwingli stood on the shore and said, "If he wishes to go under the water, let him go under." More Anabaptists were martyred *after* the Reformation than Christians were martyred during the period of Roman oppression.[8]

Luther, too, was no friend of the Anabaptists. But his debate with Zwingli stemmed from the other ordinance they both believed should endure: Communion.

The Roman Catholic doctrine of transubstantiation is based on the metaphysics of Aristotle as adopted by the Scholastics, particularly Aquinas. In this viewpoint, when the priest blesses the bread and wine, its substance is literally transformed into the body and blood of Christ, although its physical properties (taste, appearance, etc.) remain the same. Luther taught *consubstantiation*, using the analogy of an iron. When an iron is placed in a fire, the heat is comingled with the iron without the iron ceasing to be iron. For Luther, Christ is truly present in the Lord's Supper—like the fire permeates the iron—but the physical elements remain the same. Zwingli taught that "this is my body" is symbolic, and that the bread and wine are symbols, rather than literally Christ's body and blood. This was too far for Luther to go. He apparently was still hoping for reunion with Rome and believed that tolerating Zwingli would put that out of reach forever.

John Calvin and the Calvinists

The last of the three key reformers is John Calvin (1509–1564). He was born twenty-five years after Luther and Zwingli, and thus his ministry had a different character. What Luther, Zwingli, and others had begun, Calvin systematized. Where the first generation of reformers had larger-than-life personalities (in Wittenberg, Luther had been called "the wild boar"), Calvin was much more refined: the son of an attorney, trained in the humanities, and clearly shaped by the great thinkers of the past.

In 1536, at only twenty-five years of age, Calvin published the first edition of his *Institutes of the Christian Religion*, a theological textbook that would eventually rival Aquinas's *Summa Theologica* in depth and influence. Like Zwingli, Calvin viewed the church in a regional sense, but his heavenly city was Geneva, not Zurich. He broke further from the traditional position on baptism than his predecessors (but not as far as the Anabaptists), believing that baptism corresponded to circumcision as the sign of the covenant;

believing families baptized their children because their children were born into the Christian community, and converts were baptized when they entered into the community.

The difference was whether baptism was the *means* of regeneration or a *sign* of regeneration. The Anabaptists went even further, arguing that baptism was a sign of regeneration that must take place *after* regeneration.

But Calvin's greatest impact on Christianity came from his beliefs about election.

Calvin was greatly influenced by Augustine, and like Augustine, he looked at his own life prior to his conversion and believed there was no way that he would ever have been born again without God's overriding, miraculous intervention. Calvin's doctrine of salvation (soteriology) was eventually summarized by the acronym TULIP:

T – Total Depravity. Humanity's will was not merely bruised or injured by the Fall, but so totally destroyed that no one would ever choose God without first being born again.

U – Unconditional Election. God chooses who will be saved, not on the basis of any condition, whether works, foreseen faith, or ethnicity. Those who are saved are saved because of God's sovereign pleasure.

L – Limited Atonement. Jesus died only for those who were elected to be saved. This is sometimes called particular or definite atonement. To Calvin, if Jesus died for some who were not saved, then his death did not save anyone; it only provided the possibility of salvation.

I – Irresistible Grace. Those who are born again or regenerated are not given any choice to accept or reject it: Grace is irresistible. However, Calvin maintained that God still respected free will. Those who are condemned freely choose to sin; once born again, the regenerated freely choose to trust Christ.

P – Perseverance of the Saints. When someone has been born again, God keeps them by his power, and there is no possibility of their ever returning to spiritual darkness.

In Calvin's own words: "God begins his good work in us, therefore, by arousing love and desire and zeal for righteousness in our hearts; or, to speak more correctly, by bending, forming, and directing our hearts to righteousness. He completes his work, moreover, by confirming us to perseverance."[9]

Calvin's doctrine is summarized in the Heidelberg Catechism (1562) and the Westminster Confession (1646). The Puritans, who eventually left England for North America, were a particularly rigorous sect, devoted to Calvinist theology and personal purity. Calvinism is propagated today by Presbyterian, Reformed, and many Baptist churches, but it was not without its critics—one of whom we must mention: Jacobus Arminius.

Arminius (1560–1609) was born toward the end of Calvin's life, and the most important statement of his principles (the Articles of Remonstrance) wasn't written until Arminius had also died. But the conflict between Arminian and Calvinist theology continues today.

Arminians believe that Calvin's view of total depravity is too extreme. Human beings never choose God freely, but through his prevenient grace, God can give them sufficient illumination to make a free choice to accept or reject him. They view election as conditional (based on faith), atonement as sufficient for all people but applied only to those who believe, and grace as resistible (people may choose to accept or reject grace). The Articles of Remonstrance do not take a position on perseverance, saying that whether someone who deliberately committed apostasy would lose their salvation required further study. Arminians today are split over the question, though the majority deny perseverance, with many Arminian Baptists as the key exception.

Other Reformers

Other great thinkers of this period who deserve mention, though here it must be brief, include Menno Simons and John Smyth.

In 1536, Menno Simons was baptized as an Anabaptist. After a radical group of Anabaptists violently took control of the city of Munster for more than a year, his followers—the Mennonites—were an important representation of the peaceful philosophy of the majority of Anabaptists.

In 1609, John Smyth argued that there were no legitimate churches on the earth for him to receive proper baptism, and so he baptized himself before baptizing thirty-six others. He was given the nickname Se-Baptist (self-baptist), which eventually was shortened to Baptist. Smyth is generally considered to be the first Baptist. His story is interesting because he later came into contact with the Mennonites, realized there were churches *already* practicing believer's baptism, and renounced his self-baptism. He asked his congregation to do the same. Many refused, and the church split. Smyth died awaiting baptism by the Mennonites.

Other groups maintained a close connection to their traditional forms. Moscow became an independent patriarchate in 1589, splitting off from the Eastern Orthodox Church to form the Russian Orthodox Church. The Church of England declared its sovereignty from the Roman Catholic Church in 1534 when King Henry VIII instituted the Act of Supremacy. Henry intended for the church to remain basically Catholic, but with the privilege of annulling his marriage. After Henry VIII's death, Thomas Cranmer brought the Church of England more closely into alignment with Protestant principles during Edward VI's brief reign. Queen Mary I tried to return England to Roman Catholicism, and Queen Elizabeth I returned the church to Protestantism. Today, the Church of England (or the Anglican Communion) is basically Protestant in theology and Roman Catholic in structure and style.

The Counter-Reformation

Luther originally intended to reform the Catholic church while remaining within it. Though this goal proved unattainable, some of his criticisms and those of the other reformers were recognized as valid; others were rejected. Three important consequences came from the Counter-Reformation: the founding of the Jesuits, the resumption of the Inquisition, and the Council of Trent.

The Counter-Reformation was a considerable success. As church historian Bruce Shelley observes, "Faced by the rebellion of almost half of Europe, Catholicism rolled back the tide of Protestantism until by the end of the sixteenth century, Protestantism was limited roughly to the northern third of Europe, as it is today."[10]

In 1540, Ignatius Loyola was given permission from the Vatican to establish the Society of Jesus. Their primary purpose was to eliminate Protestantism, and they took to heart their authority to overthrow the "heretical" leaders of Protestant states. The Jesuits were designed to be highly mobile, and they aggressively adjusted their approach based on the culture where their missionaries and teachers served. Theologically, the most interesting legacy of the Jesuits today comes from Luis de Molina, whose *Concordia* proposed something of a middle way between Calvinist and Arminian understandings of election. This philosophy, Molinism, has been picked up by several twenty-first-century Protestants.

The Jesuits were particularly influential at the Council of Trent in 1545. There, they formally renounced all the key tenets of Protestantism. Salvation by grace through faith was rejected in favor of works cooperating with grace. Scripture alone was rejected for Scripture combined with the authority of pope, bishop, and council.

Great Works of Culture

In the background of all these conflicts, many important cultural works were produced. Foxe's *Book of Martyrs*, Milton's *Paradise Lost*, and Bunyan's *The Pilgrim's Progress* were all written during this period. Rembrandt painted the *Return of the Prodigal Son*. Saint Peter's Cathedral was rebuilt in 1506, Michelangelo painted the ceiling of the Sistine Chapel in 1512, and Harvard College was founded in 1636 as a seminary for Puritans.

It's important to remember that, while these momentous controversies were being battled by great minds, ordinary life continued to go on. Musicians, painters, and architects tried to glorify God as best they could by what they produced. Couples married, parents prayed with and for their children, and political authorities maneuvered one another for supremacy. Great works of God do not happen in a vacuum, apart from the concerns of everyday living. They happen in the midst of everyday life, and often go unnoticed at the time.

Evangelism and Expansion

During the Reformation era, the Roman Catholic Church was the primary force for the expansion of Christianity. Protestants were disorganized and focused on their own survival, and the Eastern Orthodox Church was dedicated to resisting the forces of Islam in the south. In 1549, Jesuit missionary Francis Xavier began his work in Japan. The next generation of Jesuit missionaries included Matteo Ricci and Michele Ruggieri, who went to China in 1582, where they adapted to the local culture, foreshadowing the approach Hudson Taylor would take many years later.

Boundaries of the Community

For the Catholics, communion with Rome was the essence of what identified a Christian. For the Protestants, it was faithfulness to the Scripture. But the Protestants could not agree on what that meant! Inevitably, the basic Protestant idea that people are free to interpret the Bible for themselves means that there is no definite way to establish which opinions are acceptable and which are not. To be sure, the major streams of Protestantism all accepted the first ecumenical creeds and created a common base of Christianity, but beyond that, how much tolerance should be accepted? That question remained to be answered by future generations, as the nature of state and free churches continued to develop.

Discipleship

With the technology of the printing press now highly developed, discipleship in this period depended heavily on the written word. Books such as Calvin's *Institutes* and personal letters helped shape the theology of the fledgling movements. In the routine life of the church, changes in worship style were a key practical tool for discipleship. In the Puritan churches, any element that could not be supported by the Bible was removed. (In Reformed circles, this is called the regulative principle.) Music was simple or non-existent, icons were destroyed, and the worship service centered on the sermon. In Lutheran churches, anything that could not be disproved by Scripture was at least potentially tolerated. These different approaches helped mold the understanding of authority in the lives of the churches.

11

The Revivalists

(AD 1700–AD 1900)

BENJAMIN FRANKLIN was one of the great minds of the American Revolution. When he went to hear George Whitefield preach a sermon, Franklin had resolved not to give anything to the offering Whitefield was collecting for a new orphanage in Georgia. In his unfinished *Autobiography*, Franklin describes his reaction as Whitefield preached:

> I had in my pocket a handful of copper money, three or four silver dollars, and five pistoles in gold [worth about a month's wages for a skilled laborer in that day]. As he proceeded I began to soften, and concluded to give the coppers. Another stroke of his oratory made me ashamed of that, and determined me to give the silver; and he finished so admirably that I emptied my pocket wholly into the collector's dish, gold and all.[1]

The period is marked not only by great intellectuals, but also by powerful preachers and leaders who renewed the passion of the common people.

Revival Preachers

In the first half of the eighteenth century, the American colonies were swept up in a movement known as the Great Awakening, an emotional call to a personal relationship with Christ. Jonathan Edwards (1703–1758), a Calvinist like most of the preachers of the movement, was a key leader. Edwards's most famous sermon is *Sinners in the Hands of an Angry God*. It is worth special attention because many believe it summarizes the cruelty and fear-mongering of preachers of this age, and Puritans in particular. Surely, his description of hell is vivid and powerful:

> The reason why they do not go down to hell at each moment, is not because God, in whose power they are, is not at present very angry with them; as he is with many miserable creatures now tormented in hell, who there feel and bear the fierceness of his wrath. Yea, God is a great deal more angry with great numbers that are now on earth; yea, doubtless with some who may read this book, who, it may be, are at ease, than he is with many of those who are now in the flames of hell. . . .
>
> In short they have no refuge, nothing to take hold of; all that preserves them every moment is the mere arbitrary will, and uncovenanted, unobliged forbearance of an incensed God.[2]

It would be overly simplistic to think of Edwards as purely negative and frightening. At other points in the sermon, his pastor's heart bursts through, pleading with the people in his congregation to accept Christ.

> Now you have an extraordinary opportunity, a day
> wherein Christ has thrown the door of mercy wide
> open, and stands calling, and crying with a loud voice to
> poor sinners; a day wherein many are flocking to him,
> and pressing into the kingdom of God; many are daily
> coming from the east, west, north, and south; many that
> were very lately in the same miserable condition that you
> are in, are now in a happy state, with their hearts filled
> with love to Him who has loved them, and washed them
> from their sins in his own blood, and rejoicing in hope of
> the glory of God.[3]

If Edwards was the Great Awakening's theologian, England's George Whitefield was its great orator. His preaching was extremely influential, and the huge crowds he drew helped feed the independent culture of the United States. Whitefield preached in the streets because there was no room for the crowds in any church building, but his method matched his message: Faith belongs out in the world, not just beneath a steeple. That attitude helped launch renewed missionary outreaches to Native Americans, even as the king of Denmark was sending out Lutheran missionaries to India and Greenland. Eventually, the fervor of the early revivalists cooled and the Great Awakening ended in the 1740s.

But it was the Second Great Awakening that turned the United States into a global center of missions. From the 1790s to the 1830s, Americans were called to personal evangelism and began to feel a concern for global missions. The leaders of this movement were generally Arminians, as exemplified by Charles Finney

(1792–1875), the most important preacher of the era. He invented the "anxious bench," a place for people to come and pray at the front of the hall, which was the forerunner of the altar call; and the "protracted meeting," where evangelistic services were held daily for days or weeks. Finney was controversial even in his own day, but his approach undeniably shaped modern Christianity.

Several other important evangelists were active during this period, as well. D. L. Moody (1837–1899) and Billy Sunday (1862–1935) were two influential speakers who held large evangelistic campaigns. In England, Charles Spurgeon (1834–1892) served as the pastor of the Metropolitan Tabernacle, which is often considered the first megachurch. Spurgeon's sermons were published around the world, and the pastor's college he founded substantially expanded his influence. His oratory is legendary. For instance: "Mountains, when in darkness hidden, are as real as in day, and God's love is as true to thee now as it was in thy brightest moments."[4]

But my personal favorite Spurgeon quote is one that I find as inspirational today as it must have been to those who heard it in 1875:

> If God had made you a house-cricket, and bidden you chirp, you could not do better than fulfil his will. Today he has made you a preacher, and you must abide in your vocation. If the earth should be removed, and the mountains should be cast into the midst of the sea, would that alter our duty? I trow not. Christ has sent us to preach the gospel; and if our life-work is not yet finished (and it is not), let us continue delivering our message under all circumstances till death shall silence us.[5]

Proliferation of Denominations

During the Reformation, Christianity was divided into Catholicism, Orthodoxy, Lutheranism, Calvinism, and Anabaptism. By the end of this period, the number of denominations had proliferated beyond counting, especially in the United States. Some of the groups were narrowly different from one another, some were divided over politics or race, and others are probably best not described as Christian at all. Even trying to list the major ones is beyond the scope of this book, but the conversion of the Wesley brothers and the founding of Methodism is worthwhile of mention for its impact on the broader Christian community.

While attending Oxford, Charles Wesley (1707–1788) and his friend William Morgan were disturbed by the spiritual coolness of their peers. Encouraged by Charles's brother John (1703–1791), the two began to meet "to support each other in both their studies and religious practice."[6] The group began to grow when John returned to Oxford in 1729, and soon became known, somewhat derisively, as the "Holy Club." The group practiced a strict regimen of accountability and Bible study, and later came to be called "Methodists" for their methodical pattern of discipleship.

In 1735, the Wesleys went to the American colony of Georgia to preach the gospel to the indigenous people there, but within two years they had both returned to England.

In 1738, Charles read Martin Luther's commentary on Galatians and cried out to God in prayer. He wrote in his journal that he had been brought to peace with God.

Days later, John went to a religious society meeting on Aldersgate Street and later described his experience there:

One was reading Luther's preface to the Epistle to the Romans. About a quarter before nine, while he was describing the change which God works in the heart through faith in Christ, I felt my heart strangely warmed. I felt I did trust in Christ, Christ alone, for salvation; and an assurance was given me that He had taken away my sins, even mine, and saved me from the law of sin and death.[7]

The Wesleys remained friends with George Whitefield, who had been a member of the Holy Club, and Whitefield called for their aid when his revival grew beyond what he could handle. Their theological differences were too significant, however (the Wesleys were Arminians, who taught that total sinlessness could be obtained through a second act of grace), and they eventually parted ways. But not before the Wesleys got a taste of Whitefield's radical approach of open-air preaching—which transformed their ministries.

Though John Wesley never intended to form a separate denomination but merely hoped to provide a stronger spiritual life within the Church of England, he and his followers were gradually forced into their own denomination. As a result of Wesley's skill at preaching and organization, at his death there were almost five hundred Methodist preachers and about 115,000 members of Methodist congregations between the United States and Britain.

Cultural Development

While some reached the masses for Christ by their powerful sermons, others "preached" through music. Along with Johann Sebastian Bach, who was born the same year, George Frideric Handel was one of several well-known musical geniuses of his time. One of his innovations, the English oratorio, was a Bible story expressed through a libretto. It was a controversial technique at the time, and he suffered great financial distress until he produced what may be the greatest example of all: *Messiah*. Even those with no interest in classical music usually recognize the "Hallelujah Chorus," though they may not recognize how sincerely the composer meant it as an act of worship.

Many of the best-known hymns of history were written during this period, as well. Charles Wesley, a gifted poet, wrote thousands of hymns, including some of the world's greatest: "Hark! The Herald Angels Sing," "Love Divine, All Loves Excelling," "Christ the Lord Is Risen Today," and "O for a Thousand Tongues to Sing." The final verse of his "And Can It Be" demonstrates both his theological insight and his poetic skill:

No condemnation now I dread;
Jesus, and all in Him, is mine;
Alive in Him, my living Head;
And clothed in righteousness divine,
Bold I approach the eternal throne,
And claim the crown, through Christ my own.

Isaac Watts, a British clergyman, is considered the father of English hymnody. Some of Watts's hymns are still regularly used in worship today. "When I Survey the Wondrous Cross" was included in *Hymns and Spiritual Songs*, and "O God, Our Help in Ages Past" was included in *The Psalms of David Imitated in the Language of the New Testament*, in which Watts paraphrased almost every Psalm to explicitly reflect the revelation of the New Testament.

Another popular hymnal was *Olney Hymns* by John Newton and William Cowper. Newton is best known for his conversion from slave trader to pastor and for authoring "Amazing Grace."

Evangelism and Expansion

This period was the golden age of Protestant missions. Throughout the known world, missionaries were recruited, funds were raised, and the footprint of Christianity was vastly expanded. This was made possible by the increased organization of missionary work and by improvements in transportation technology. A man on foot in the days of Alexander the Great was not much different from a man on foot in the days of Martin Luther. But the development of better ships and improvements in production from the Industrial Revolution made outreach feasible to an extent that would have been unattainable before.

Hudson Taylor (1832–1905) wrote that "China is not to be won for Christ by quiet, ease-loving men and women,"[8] and Taylor himself would not have been disqualified by that standard. He assimilated into Chinese culture, dressed in the local style, and traveled into the interior of China to reach the people. Catholic missionaries to China, such as Matteo Ricci and Michele Ruggieri, had utilized this approach three centuries before, but for Protestant missionaries it was a radical idea.

When poor health forced him to return to England, Taylor continued his work by translating the Bible into Chinese and organizing the China Inland Mission. The time away proved to be enormously important, even if Taylor would not have chosen it. By the time of his death, thousands of missionaries were serving in China.

In 1812, Adoniram Judson left the United States for Calcutta as a Congregational missionary. On the boat to India, however, he became persuaded that the Baptist position on baptism was correct, and he lost his financial backing at home. Baptists in America answered his call for aid, and the first Baptist mission organization was founded to meet the need. When the British East

India Company forced Judson out of India, preventing him from accomplishing his planned work there, William Carey (a Baptist missionary to India) convinced him to go to Burma, where he spent the rest of his life.

David Livingstone (1813–1873) sailed for Africa in 1840, and tried for years to be a conventional missionary, working in mission stations and having people come to him. He had little success. Finally, he became an explorer, taking the gospel with him wherever he went. He worked to undermine the slave trade, and his compassion for the people of Africa blossomed at a time when many other Europeans seemed to have no respect for them.

Boundaries of the Community

The Roman Catholic Church continued to emphasize doctrines that Protestants found reprehensible. In 1854, Pope Pius IX proclaimed the Immaculate Conception of Mary as dogma, asserting that the mother of Jesus was free from the stain of original sin. In 1870, the First Vatican Council decreed that when speaking officially on matters of faith (*ex cathedra*), the pope was infallible. Though a rapprochement between the Protestants and Rome was already almost inconceivable, this doctrinal commitment drew an even bolder boundary between the two.

Among Protestants, the explosion of denominations shows that boundaries were sometimes drawn over minor differences; but the work of united missionary societies proved that these boundaries could sometimes be overcome for a common goal. Distinctions were in flux as doctrinal systems were refined and debates continued. The boundaries of Christianity were drawn differently by different groups, but the general tenor from the Great Awakenings and the rising religious liberty in the West was toward a community of personal faith.

Discipleship

In addition to the small-group strategies of the Methodist movement, discipleship during this period was shaped by the invention of Sunday school. Most of the credit for this innovation goes to Englishman Robert Raikes, who may not have originated the idea but certainly popularized it. He believed that educating children and teaching them the Bible would benefit both the children and society. Thus, in 1780, he recruited four women to teach the poor children on Sundays. Soon, in response to the apparently improved behavior of the children, Sunday schools were popularized throughout the Church of England. Shortly after, the same idea was picked up by other groups around the world.

12

The Century of Global War

(AD 1900S)

DIETRICH BONHOEFFER was a pastor and theological professor in Berlin when the Nazis first rose to power in 1933. Bonhoeffer publicly challenged them and became a leader among the German Protestant resistance to Adolf Hitler's attempts to weaponize the churches of Germany. In 1937, he published *The Cost of Discipleship*, in which he observed, "When Christ calls a man, he bids him come and die."[1]

In 1939, Bonhoeffer fled to New York City; but overcome by conscience, he stayed only two weeks before returning to Germany, where he continued to oppose the Nazi regime until he was arrested and jailed for his resistance efforts on April 5, 1943.

In July 1944, Colonel Claus von Stauffenberg attempted to assassinate Hitler and failed. Bonhoeffer's involvement in the plot was eventually discovered, and he was executed on April 9, 1945, just three weeks before Hitler committed suicide.

The twentieth century was a time of tremendous turmoil. Two World Wars, a Cold War that seemed to threaten the survival of humanity, and the collapse of ancient empires were clearly visible signs that things were changing. Just as surely, there was a battle for the meaning of Christianity itself. The modernists, building on Enlightenment principles, sought to redefine Christianity's relationship to miracles and the authority of the Bible. At the other end of the spectrum, the burgeoning Pentecostal movement called for a return to personal holiness and belief in modern-day signs and wonders, in an echo of Tertullian and the Montanists over 1,500 years before. This was a century of global war, fought with both bullets and ink.

Conservatism and Liberalism

One of the great struggles of the twentieth century was not between denominations but within the realm of theology. With German higher criticism questioning the authorship and text of the Bible, the challenges of evolutionary theory and geology to traditional understandings of Genesis set the Bible as the battleground. Wrestling with the social impact of Christianity in light of emerging ideologies, such as Marxism, caused some to fundamentally question the nature of sin. Liberal theologians, including Rudolf Bultmann (1884–1976), argued that the "myths" of Christianity that prevented modern people from believing needed to be jettisoned so they could receive the essence of the gospel.

In response, conservatives published a series of books called *The Fundamentals*, arguing for the centrality of the authority of the Bible, the virgin birth, the bodily resurrection of Jesus, and the need for personal conversion. In 1923, American J. Gresham Machen, a leader in the Fundamentalist movement, wrote *Christianity and Liberalism*, in which he famously argued that liberalism was a different faith from Christianity:

> In the sphere of religion, in particular, the present time
> is a time of conflict; the great redemptive religion which
> has always been known as Christianity is battling against
> a totally diverse type of religious belief, which is only
> the more destructive of the Christian faith because it
> makes use of traditional Christian terminology. This
> modern non-redemptive religion is called "modernism" or
> "liberalism."[2]

Though the controversy between the Fundamentalists and the Modernists divided denominations and resulted in high-profile controversies, it took a back seat to cultural upheaval from the Great Depression to the end of World War II. By then, the meaning of the word *fundamentalist* had shifted from referring to "the fundamentals of Christianity" to a connotation of "closed-minded traditionalism." Trying to dissociate themselves from the fundamentalist label, many in the movement adopted the name *evangelical*, from the Greek word for "gospel."

The evangelicals often left historical denominations to form new, conservative denominations they believed were more faithful to Scripture. One prominent exception to this pattern was the case of the Southern Baptist Convention, the largest Protestant denomination in the United States, where the conservatives effectively pushed the liberals out.

The gradual movement of the denomination's stance on abortion is representative of the shifts taking place within the denomination.

In June 1971, the Southern Baptist Convention's messengers met in St. Louis and passed ten resolutions. The most surprising from our current perspective is the resolution on abortion, which ends with these words: "Be it further resolved, that we call upon Southern Baptists to work for legislation that will allow the possibility of abortion under such conditions as rape, incest, clear evidence of severe fetal deformity, and carefully ascertained evidence of the likelihood of damage to the emotional, mental, and physical health of the mother."[3]

That resolution was reaffirmed in June 1974, explicitly calling the earlier vote "a middle ground between the extreme of abortion on demand and the opposite extreme of all abortion as murder."[4] By 1976, the tone had changed substantially: "Every decision for an abortion, for whatever reason, must necessarily involve the decision to terminate the life of an innocent human being."[5] Finally, in 1980, the Southern Baptist Convention resolved "that we favor appropriate legislation and/or a constitutional amendment prohibiting abortion except to save the life of the mother."[6]

God's Word in Man's Tongue, Updated

From the time of William Tyndale, most English Bibles were simply revisions of his work, shaped by the text developed by Erasmus. Over time, new manuscript discoveries provided scholars with more information to help them reconstruct the original text, and these new editions formed the foundation for a new generation of translations.

In 1960, translators produced the New American Standard Bible, utilizing a strict word-for-word approach in an effort to preserve the original structure of the text. The NASB, and its subsequent updates, is still favored by many Bible students for the way it makes Hebrew and Greek syntax and word choice obvious, though sometimes at the expense of fluid English.

In 1971, Tyndale House Publishers produced *The Living Bible*, which paraphrased the Bible text in contemporary language that could easily be understood, even by children.

In 1978, the New International Version was published, using a similar "dynamic equivalence" approach as *The Living Bible*, while attempting to adhere to the literal form of the text.

In 1982, the New King James Version provided a new translation of the traditional KJV text; and in 1996, Tyndale House published the New Living Translation, converting the earlier paraphrase into a translation from the original languages.

New Tools and Techniques

Billy Graham (1918–2018) was ordained as a Southern Baptist pastor but served only briefly as a local church pastor. His ministry was centered on evangelistic meetings in stadiums around the world, leading to a long-running radio program and a series of books. Graham's place as one of the greatest evangelists in history was made clear during his first series of tent revivals (he called them crusades before that term fell into disfavor) in Los Angeles in 1949. Over eight weeks, attendance totaled 350,000, with 3,000 professions of faith in Jesus. His sermons from that time are reminiscent of Jonathan Edwards—a mixture of warning about eternal judgment and a pastoral plea to repent before it's too late:

> You're going to cry out, but your cry is going to be too late. You're going to say, "Oh God, have mercy upon me," but there'll be no mercy. God said, "I'll be laughing at your calamity, I'll be mocking you, I'll be laughing at you, and I won't answer your prayer in that day because you rejected Jesus Christ, and you turned down God, and you didn't accept Christ as your personal Savior." . . .

> When the Lord Jesus Christ died on the cross of
> Calvary, the work of salvation was complete, and God
> said: "Believe. Put your faith in Him."[7]

Graham's effectiveness came from a willingness to adapt to new techniques and technologies. He mimicked the style of the radio and television personalities of his day and spoke to people in plain language. The first Christian TV broadcasts began as early as 1940, but Graham knew how to leverage the mass media of his day for the gospel in a way few others have been able to emulate. His charisma and integrity helped him become an advisor to several presidents and helped make conservative theology more visible in the mainstream culture.

Around the same time, but at the opposite end of the theological spectrum, was Robert Schuller (1926–2015), a pastor with the Reformed Church in America. In 1955, at a Southern California drive-in movie theater, Schuller began preaching from the roof of the snack bar to a congregation gathered in their cars. Schuller's pitch was, "Come as you are in the family car." Though he faced opposition for preaching at a venue that many conservative Christians would avoid, he had tremendous success reaching the community. When he invited another RCA pastor, Norman Vincent Peale (best known as the author of *The Power of Positive Thinking*), to preach at one of his services, he was moved by Peale's positive, encouraging approach and decided to model his ministry on it. Schuller's sermons sounded very little like Billy Graham's warnings about God laughing at the calamity of the lost on the Day of Judgment:

> The me I see is the me I will be. . . . How do *you* see
> yourself today? How do you rate your self-confidence? . . .

Well, there are three major emotional demons that
I believe block the burst of faith in life that could cause
us to become possibility thinkers. The three emotional
demons are inferiority, inadequacy, and incompetence. In
all of these three negative emotions, *you* can find release,
and with the release, you'll begin to think it's possible.[8]

These two sermons reflect very different flavors of American
Christianity, and both have their advocates and critics. Robert
Schuller also used the cultural tools of the modern era with incredible effectiveness. His television program, *The Hour of Power*, was
watched by twenty million viewers each week, and the ambitious
Crystal Cathedral (the largest glass structure in the world when it
was completed in 1982) drew people for its architecture as well as
for the church services.

A New Kind of Music

Another cultural trend that gained traction in the late 1960s came
to be known as the Jesus Movement—fueled by church leaders
(notably Chuck Smith with Calvary Chapel) targeting young
people. The movement tended to be charismatic—that is, with
an emphasis on spiritual gifts—and like many previous reform
efforts, challenged the wealth and casual lifestyles of established
churches.

Churches in the Jesus Movement called for spiritual revival
and rejected traditions about hair length for men, clothing
styles, and music. These churches began to replace the singing
of hymns with new Christian songs written in a pop style. The
lyrics focused more on the imminent than the transcendent,
which aligned well with the movement's emphasis on a personal
relationship with Jesus.

Though initially this contemporary music was found mostly in youth-oriented churches, it gradually spread into more established churches as well, often meeting with substantial opposition. Some churches, especially those with liturgical roots, retained their traditional music, and some churches blended the different styles together. Conflict over musical styles sometimes resulted in Protestant churches dividing or holding a separate "rock 'n' roll" service, but eventually, the so-called worship wars were won decisively by an emerging genre known as Contemporary Christian Music (CCM), which was profoundly shaped by the popular music of the day.

Music that is imminent and personal has become the norm, though traditional hymns (some dating back to Charles Wesley and his contemporaries) have held their own in some congregations, while others have been adapted to the contemporary style. The growing emphasis on the imminent feeds into the individualism of our culture and reflects the declining sense of the transcendent in Western culture.

Like many of the ecclesiastical controversies down through the ages, there is no simple answer. As always, Christians must use the best tools available, with the greatest wisdom possible, without compromising their faithfulness to God. Still, it is tragically ironic that, with all the problems in the world for which the gospel is the answer, few things have divided modern evangelicals more than preferences about musical styles.

The Transformation of Roman Catholicism

In March 1939, Cardinal Eugenio Pacelli (1876–1958) became Pope Pius XII. In a different era, Pius might have been considered a success for his gracious personal demeanor and gentle reforms that seemed to annoy liberals and conservatives equally. He unilaterally declared the Assumption of Mary (that she bodily ascended into heaven) as dogma, and it was during his papacy that Mother Teresa's Missionaries of Charity were formally recognized. Instead, his legacy was defined by his response to events beyond his control.

Six months after Pius XII was elected, Nazi Germany invaded Poland, igniting World War II. Pius challenged the Nazis only vaguely in his public remarks, and some called him "Hitler's Pope." One might say that is an unfair accusation against a man who secretly gave information to the Allies and instructed priests to provide shelter and aid to Jews. But he was certainly less assertive than many people would have liked.

When Pius's successor was named—the seventy-six-year-old Angelo Roncalli (1881–1963)—many expected him to be little more than a transitional pope. But Pope John XXIII had other ideas. After only a few months in office, he announced plans to convene a new ecumenical council to modernize the church.

The Second Vatican Council (1962–1965), often called Vatican II, became probably the most important Catholic council since Trent. It allowed a liturgy in the local vernacular instead of Latin; lay people could now receive both the bread and the wine in Communion; social work in the developing world was emphasized; and there was a new openness to seeing other Christian denominations as "separated brethren."

John died before the council's work was completed, but Paul VI (1897–1978) announced immediately that it would continue. When the dust settled in 1965, the council had found common ground between the conservatives and liberals for each issue it considered. A few groups splintered from Rome over the council's decrees, but their numbers were small.

One last twentieth-century pope should be mentioned. John Paul II (1920–2005) was the second-longest-serving pope in history, from 1978–2005. He traveled more than every preceding pope combined, was fluent in eight languages, and was the first pope to visit a synagogue and a mosque. Theologically, he was more conservative than John XXIII or Paul VI, but he was charismatic and worked actively for the rights of people around the world. He worked aggressively against the Communist movement and is often credited with helping negotiate the peaceful fall of the USSR, even as he criticized the excesses of the wealthy capitalist West. John Paul was Polish, and the first non-Italian to serve as pope in more than four hundred years. He was formally canonized as a saint on April 27, 2014, less than a decade after his death—one of the fastest canonizations in history. The primary cloud that hangs over his reign is the sexual abuse scandal, which we'll discuss in the next chapter.

Evangelism and Expansion

During the twentieth century, one of the greatest threats to Christian evangelism was the anti-religious sentiments of the Communists. From the beginnings of the Soviet Union in 1917, religion has been under attack. Thousands of believers were killed early in the Communist Revolution, largely because of the close entanglement between the Russian Orthodox Church and the czarist government. Initially, evangelicals were given more latitude, on the principle that the enemy of my enemy is my friend. But they, too, were eventually targeted for destruction. Officially, Article 52 of the Soviet Constitution guarantees religious freedom, but this was never enforced. There was little religious freedom until the reforms brought by Mikhail Gorbachev shortly before the breakup of the Soviet Union.

In 1952, all foreign missionaries were expelled from China, and Chinese church leader Watchman Nee was arrested. In 1972, the first reports of secret house churches were leaked, although they do not appear to have gained substantial influence until 1978. In 1982, the Chinese government released Document 19, which officially provided some tolerance to religious groups, though actual practice is, at best, inconsistent. In China, some official churches are tolerated, but the real growth remains in the secret house churches. Tertullian's observation seems to hold true: The blood of the martyrs is the seed of the church.

The final major issue we'll discuss from the twentieth century is the church growth movement. In *The Bridges of God* (1955), veteran missionary Donald McGavran (1897–1990) establishes that people are brought to faith in groups, and that ignoring the sociological elements of conversion leads to poor results. McGavran looked at mission outposts that provided humanitarian aid without resulting in much personal faith and called instead for a movement that would reach new believers and organize multiplying churches.

When McGavran coined the term "church growth," he was primarily concerned with missions in unreached people groups, but Western readers found his ideas effective in local churches as well, and a movement was born. McGavran's intellectual heir was C. Peter Wagner, but by the 1980s, the key leadership in the movement had transitioned from seminary professors to successful pastors. One key example is Rick Warren (b. 1954), whose book *The Purpose Driven Church* became an important rallying point for the movement.

Warren argued that most churches are driven by the wrong kinds of things, and thus produce the wrong kinds of results. After challenging churches that are driven by tradition, personality, finances, programs, buildings, events, and seekers, he wrote, "What is needed today are churches that are driven by purpose instead of by other forces."[9] Warren's *purposes*—fellowship, discipleship, worship, ministry, and evangelism—echoed McGavran's concerns from a generation before. Though Warren didn't use the same language, his advice to churches to target evangelism demographically was an appeal to reach people groups.[10] The church growth movement fueled the modern megachurch phenomenon, which was successful through the twentieth century, although it eventually plateaued.

Boundaries of the Community

The twentieth century was the century of organization. In 1910, the Edinburgh Conference (World Missionary Conference) sought to arrange for Christian unity in world evangelism, but its most lasting effect has been the ecumenical movement. The conference passed a resolution "to plant in each non-Christian nation one undivided Church of Christ."[11] Though this lofty goal has not yet been achieved, the World Missionary Conference became the forerunner for the World Council of Churches, an organization that continues to seek Christian unity so that the world can be reached for Christ. Some evangelical critics of the WCC have wondered what the purpose is in reaching the world if important theological distinctions are dissolved in the process. Ecumenism experienced its heyday in the mid-twentieth century, with dozens of denominational mergers. One of the more prominent examples in the United States was the creation of the United Methodist Church in 1968. Now, less than sixty years later, United Methodism itself is splitting. The challenges of ecumenism are steep.

Discipleship

In 1906, African American preacher William J. Seymour started holding prayer meetings in a dilapidated industrial building at

312 Azusa Street in Los Angeles. Seymour preached that the baptism of the Holy Spirit was always accompanied by speaking in tongues (something he had been taught in Charles Parham's Bible School in Houston), and soon the gift of tongues took hold in his congregation. Large interracial crowds began to gather three times a day, and participants reported miracles and healings.[12]

The Azusa Street Revival burned hot for three years before it began to decline, but the modern Pentecostal movement was born. The Holiness Movement, a call to greater devotion within the Methodist Church, became the foundation of Pentecostalism and began to associate Wesley's doctrine of a second work of grace with speaking in tongues. Numerous Pentecostal denominations were formed, but by the 1960s, the movement had seeped into established denominations as well. Believers of all doctrinal affiliations began Pentecostal practices within their existing traditions, in what came to be called the Charismatic Movement. The question of whether the spiritual gifts of the New Testament are available to believers today or if they ceased during the first century was a key issue in discipleship. Are there two classes of believers, those who have received a second blessing and those who have not?

Another controversy that developed rapidly in the twentieth century was the question of whether women could be ordained. There were a few examples of ordination of women in loosely organized congregations during the Protestant Reformation, but they were rare. Around 1890, more denominations gradually began ordaining women, but the practice did not become widespread outside of Pentecostal churches until the 1960s.[13] In the United States, Methodist and Presbyterian women were given access to full ordination in 1956 (though women had long been preaching in Methodism).[14] The first woman was ordained as a priest in the Church of England in 1994.[15]

Are men and women equal in dignity but distinct in role? Or are men and women in the modern era both called by God to the same work and opportunities? Ordination is merely a specific instance of the broader question of complementarianism versus egalitarianism, and the debate continues.

13

The Information Era

(AD 2000–PRESENT)

In 2006, Gallup determined that 42 percent of Americans favored same-sex marriage. By 2015, the number was 60 percent, and in 2022, it was 71 percent.[1] It is difficult to think of another period in history in which public opinion on a major issue changed so dramatically over such a brief span of time. But the velocity of change has accelerated so quickly in our modern society that it's hard to keep up. The rapid development of technology is obviously a major factor in this change.

In 1998, Nobel Prize–winning economist Paul Krugman famously claimed that the internet was a fad, and its effect on our daily lives would be comparable to the invention of the fax machine.

This seems laughable now, but only because the power of computers and the speed of the internet have increased to levels that are nearly unfathomable. People are connected in new ways, business models are continually being rewritten, and it is clear that there is no turning back—we have been fully immersed in the Information Era. Events, opinions, and perspectives that once might only have been known within a limited subculture are now instant news for anyone with a cell phone. Turmoil in one part of the world cannot be contained there. Everything now is potentially global, or viral. It is in this brave new world that God's people are tasked with preaching the original, unchanging gospel.

Leadership Scandals

In the twentieth century, megachurches were in style. But toward the end of that era and up to the present, their rates of growth have stalled, and many large churches have shifted from a single large campus to multiple sites. The reasons for this are complex, and they reflect both broad social trends and others specific to the church, but a handful of high-profile scandals provide some insight.

In 1996, Mark Driscoll (b. 1970) cofounded Mars Hill Church, which grew into a megachurch in Seattle. Within a few years, he was extremely popular and influential, serving on major boards, preaching at conferences, and writing books that appeared on the bestseller list. By 2013, average weekly attendance was more than 12,000.

Then, it all came crashing down. Due to personal character flaws (including charges of plagiarism, online bullying, and manipulating sales to claim the title of bestselling author), he resigned in disgrace. The Mars Hill campuses split into independent churches, but reports indicate that huge numbers of people were disillusioned and abandoned the faith completely.

Then Bill Hybels, the founder of influential Willow Creek Community Church near Chicago, resigned in April 2018 after serious accusations of moral failure were made against him (although he denied the claims). Willow Creek's attendance, too, has suffered serious decline.

There are plenty of other examples, but these make the point of a basic vulnerability in the megachurch model. When there is a failure at the top, the ripple effects are massive. Churches have moved toward more flexible, multisite arrangements, with more autonomy for each campus, allowing leaders to be raised up locally, and preventing one catastrophic failure from causing harm to so many.

Other Scandals

Scandals have not been limited to individual churches. The Roman Catholic Church and the Southern Baptist Convention have faced serious accusations of covering up and mishandling sexual abuse by Christian leaders. Both groups have responded with plans to identify offenders and prevent future abuse, but egalitarians see these failures as evidence of the basic inadequacy of the complementarian approach to ministry. When too much power is consolidated by gender, they argue, abuse is much more likely. Complementarians argue that it is not their theology of gender that is causing the problem, pointing to similar sexual abuse in progressive places such as Hollywood. The reaction of non-Christians is probably much simpler: Where is the power that is supposed to change lives?

Modern developments in technology mean that stories that once might have been covered up or gone unnoticed are much more difficult to hide. Anyone with a computer can write a blog post or send a tweet, and personal testimonies are available almost anywhere on earth in an instant. Perhaps this kind of thing has been going on for generations but was unknown to anyone except the participants and the Judge of all the earth. Regardless, when church leaders have fallen into obvious sin, it has always caused frustration and discontent, whether during the Protestant Reformation or the Information Era.

COVID-19 and Beyond

In early 2020, the world became aware of a new virus that caused an infection called COVID-19. It soon reached pandemic status, resulting in worldwide lockdowns where people were encouraged or commanded to stay home to avoid infection. In many places, churches closed—either voluntarily or due to government guidelines. A generation ago, this would have been a catastrophic development for most churches. But the ready availability of technology—from inexpensive video cameras to online meeting forums and widespread high-speed internet access—meant that churches could continue to "meet" without meeting in person. Even small churches were able to hold services by video call and maintain contact with their membership during the lockdown. Many churches began streaming their services online and have continued.

Technology is both a blessing and a curse for Christians. It makes Christian community and education much easier, but that convenience can become a curse when it facilitates a lack of personal connection and commitment. Striking the balance between removing unnecessary obstacles and compromising on essentials is as old as Acts 15. Yes, online services allow someone to hear preaching, reflect on worship music, and be encouraged, even when they are unable to leave home. But there is no way to "greet each other with a sacred kiss" on Zoom (Romans 16:16). It's hard to practice Matthew 18:15—"If another believer sins against you, go privately and point out the offense"—on Twitter. Christians have gathered together from the earliest times, even as they waited in the upper room for the coming of the Holy Spirit, or as they hid in houses during the Decian persecution. There is something precious—and necessary—about being *together*. Determining the proper role of online worship will be the job of wise theologians for years to come, if they are willing to take up the task.

One more effect of COVID-19: It seems certain that the concept of social distancing that was enforced at the height of the pandemic will combine with other trends working against megachurches and neighborhood churches alike. Some might say that COVID *caused* these new challenges that churches now face, but it seems more likely to have accelerated trends that were already in place.

East and West

The fastest-growing religious sector in Europe and North America at the beginning of the twenty-first century was the "nones," people with no particular religious affiliation. Atheism, agnosticism, and a kind of official secularism have reshaped the Western world, and the places that once were thoroughly Christianized are now increasingly post-Christian. In the developing world, on the other hand, Christianity is resurgent. Churches that were established by the great wave of missionary work two centuries ago are taking their own authority and expressing the faith based on their own understanding. Even more importantly, these nations are experiencing a surge in indigenous church planting, often by design but also of necessity, as their former benefactors decline. The places where Christianity was strongest in the early centuries of our modern era are now gaining strength.

The Ends of the Earth

Even as we rejoice that certain regions are hearing the gospel again after growing cold, we must remember that the gospel has not yet reached the entire world—though Christians are still trying. On

May 12, 2020, Joyce Lin lost her life when her airplane crashed into Lake Sentani in Papua, Indonesia. She had two engineering degrees from MIT and a decade of service as an officer in the US Air Force, but she gave her life as a pilot with Mission Aviation Fellowship, a team that takes the gospel to remote people groups.[2] Today, along with groups such as Wycliffe Bible Translators (founded in 1934) and an army of missionaries known only to God, the gospel is still being sacrificially carried to those who have not yet heard. The Joshua Project, at the time of this writing, lists more than 4,000 people groups in which none of the population identifies as Christian. The estimated 7,414 people groups with a Christian population of 5 percent or less make up 42.3 percent of the population of the world—some 3.3 billion people. There is still work to be done, but the words of Jesus from Acts 1:8 still ring true: "You will receive power when the Holy Spirit comes upon you. And you will be my witnesses, telling people about me everywhere—in Jerusalem, throughout Judea, in Samaria, and to the ends of the earth."

The story continues.

Notes

PREFACE

1. Matthew 28:18-20.

CHAPTER 1: THE SETTING OF CHRISTIAN HISTORY

1. See for example, Bill T. Arnold and Bryan E. Beyer, *Encountering the Old Testament: A Christian Survey* (Grand Rapids, MI: Baker, 1999), 475; John Mark Terry, *Evangelism: A Concise History* (Nashville, TN: Broadman & Holman, 1994), 3; Justo L. González, *The Story of Christianity: Volume I: The Early Church to the Dawn of the Reformation* (San Francisco: HarperSanFrancisco, 1984), 7.

2. Karen Brooks, "Officials Triple Number of Homes Charred in Texas Fire," Reuters, September 8, 2011, https://www.reuters.com/article/us-texas-wildfires-idUSTRE78426D20110908.

3. Alexander allowed the free practice of the Jewish faith, according to Josephus in *Antiquities of the Jews*, 11.337–338. Everyday life in Jerusalem was probably not seriously affected for quite some time. See Paolo Sacchi, *The History of the Second Temple Period* (Sheffield, UK: Sheffield Academic, 2000), 160–161.

4. Josephus, *Antiquities of the Jews*, book 12, sec. 4–5, in *Josephus: Jewish Antiquities*, vol. V: books 12–13, trans. Ralph Marcus (Cambridge, MA: Harvard University Press, 1943), 2–5.

5. Michael D. Marlowe, ed., "The Translators to the Reader" (Bible Research: Internet Resources for Students of Scripture, n.d.), http://www.bible-researcher.com/kjvpref.html.

6. Mary T. Boatwright et al., *The Romans: From Village to Empire*, 2nd ed. (New York: Oxford University Press, 2012), 95–97.

7. Boatwright et al., *Romans*, 167.

8. Craig Ott and Stephen J. Strauss, *Encountering Theology of Mission* (Grand Rapids, MI: Baker Academic, 2010), 23.

9. John Madden, "Slavery in the Roman Empire: Numbers and Origins," *Classics Ireland*, vol. 3 (1996), 109–128. See also "Roman Slavery," UNRV Roman History, accessed September 21, 2022, https://www.unrv.com /slavery.php.

10. "Abodah Zarah," 2:1, I.5–IV.1, in Jacob Neusner, *The Jerusalem Talmud: A Translation and Commentary* (Peabody, MA: Hendrickson, 2008).

11. Lee I. Levine, "The Nature and Origin of the Palestinian Synagogue Reconsidered," *Journal of Biblical Literature* 115, no. 3 (Autumn 1996): 438–440.

CHAPTER 2: THE APOSTOLIC PERIOD

1. Flavius Josephus, *The Wars of the Jews*, book II, ch. VII, trans. Roger L'Estrange (Manchester, UK: J. Harrop, 1767), 99–100.

2. John 18:36.

3. Compare this with Galatians 3:13: "But Christ has rescued us from the curse pronounced by the law. When he was hung on the cross, he took upon himself the curse for our wrongdoing. For it is written in the Scriptures, 'Cursed is everyone who is hung on a tree.'"

4. *The Life of Flavius Josephus*, in Flavius Josephus, *The Works of Josephus: Complete and Unabridged*, trans. William Whiston (Peabody, MA: Hendrickson, 1987), 25.

5. Thomas R. Schreiner, *Exegetical Commentary on the New Testament: Galatians* (Grand Rapids, MI: Zondervan, 2010), 102–103.

6. Harold B. Mattingly, "The Origin of the Name *Christiani*," *Journal of Theological Studies*, vol. 9, no. 1 (April 1958), 31, https://doi.org/10 .1093/jts/IX.1.26.

7. Suetonius, *The Deified Claudius* 25.4, Book V of *Lives of the Caesars*, in *Suetonius, with an English Translation* by J. C. Rolfe, Loeb Classical Library 38 (Cambridge, MA: Harvard University Press, 1914), 2:52–53.

8. John Bradner, "Paul's Physical Appearance According to Early Christian Literature and Iconography," *Hartford Quarterly* 7, no. 2 (1967): 58–73.

9. Walter Gustafson, "Christ the Perfect Servant in the Gospel of Mark (1): Introduction," *Truth & Tidings*, vol. 65, no. 1, January 2014.

10. Eusebius, *Ecclesiastical History*, 3.1.2, trans. C. F. Cruse (Peabody, MA: Hendrickson, 1998), 67.

CHAPTER 3: THE POST-APOSTOLIC PERIOD

1. Flavius Josephus, *The Wars of the Jews*, 14.6, in Flavius Josephus, *The Works of Josephus: Complete and Unabridged*, trans. William Whiston (Peabody, MA: Hendrickson, 1987), 616.

2. Roswell D. Hitchcock and Francis Brown, trans. and eds., *The Teaching of the Twelve Apostles*, revised and enlarged edition (London: John C. Nimmo, 1885), 3–5. Italics in the original. Biblical cross-references have been added in brackets.

3. Angelo Di Berardino, Thomas C. Oden, and Joel C. Elowsky, *Encyclopedia of Ancient Christianity*, vol. 1 (Downers Grove, IL: InterVarsity Press, 2014), 475.

4. Pliny the Younger, *Letters*, 10.96.7–8, trans. B. Radice, in Pliny the Younger, *Letters, Volume II: Books 8–10. Panegyricus* (Cambridge, MA: Harvard University Press, 1969).

5. See also Mark 9:41; 1 Peter 4:16; Revelation 3:12; and Ignatius, *Epistle of Ignatius to the Ephesians*, 7:1, http://www.earlychristianwritings.com/text /ignatius-ephesians-lightfoot.html.

6. Pliny the Younger, *Letters*, 10.97.

7. John Mark Terry, Ebbie C. Smith, and Justice Anderson, *Missiology: An Introduction to the Foundations, History, and Strategies of World Missions* (Nashville, TN: Broadman & Holman, 1998), 167.

8. Michael Green, *Evangelism in the Early Church* (Grand Rapids, MI: Eerdmans, 2004), 16.

9. Eusebius, *Ecclesiastical History*, 4.5.1–2, trans. C. F. Cruse (Peabody, MA: Hendrickson, 1998), 111.

10. Donald A. McGavran, *The Bridges of God: A Study in the Strategy of Missions* (Eugene, OR: Wipf & Stock, 2005), 32.

11. Everett Ferguson, *Church History: From Christ to Pre-Reformation*, vol. 1 (Grand Rapids, MI: Zondervan, 2005), 47–49.

12. Ignatius, *Epistle of Ignatius to the Ephesians*, 7:2, http://www .earlychristianwritings.com/text/ignatius-ephesians-lightfoot.html.

CHAPTER 4: THE APOLOGIST PERIOD

1. "#103: Polycarp's Martyrdom," Christian History Institute, https:// christianhistoryinstitute.org/study/module/polycarp; "St. Polycarp of Smyrna," Catholic News Agency, https://www.catholicnewsagency.com /saint/st-polycarp-of-smyrna-156.

2. 1 John 5:21. The NLT gives this literal translation in a footnote.

3. F. L. Cross and Elizabeth A. Livingstone, eds., "Marcion," in *The Oxford Dictionary of the Christian Church* (Oxford; New York: Oxford University Press, 2005), 1040.

4. Justin Martyr, "First Apology," 1.26, trans. and ed. Leslie William Barnard, in *The First and Second Apologies*, Ancient Christian Writers, vol. 56 (Mahwah, NJ: Paulist Press, 1997), 41, https://archive.org/details /firstsecondapolo00just_0/page/40/mode/2up.

5. Justin Martyr, "First Apology," 1.31, 44.

6. Cassius Dio, *Epitome* 67.14, in *Dio's Roman History*, vol. 8, trans. Earnest Cary (London: William Heinemann, 1925), 349, https://archive.org /details/diosromanhistory08cassuoft/page/348/mode/2up.

7. Justin Martyr, "First Apology," 1.6, 26.

8. Antti Marjanen, "Montanism: Egalitarian Ecstatic 'New Prophecy,'" in *A Companion to Second-Century Christian "Heretics,"* vol. 76, eds. Antti Marjanen and Petri Luomanen (Boston: Brill, 2008), 185–186.

9. Marjanen, "Montanism," 188.

10. John Wesley, *Sermons on Several Occasions* (New York: Lane & Scott, 1848), 110.

11. See particularly note 2 in Adolf von Harnack, *History of Dogma*, ed. T. K. Cheyne and A. B. Bruce, vol. 2 (Boston: Roberts Brothers, 1897), 95; J. M. Carroll, *The Trail of Blood* (Pensacola, FL: West Florida Baptist Institute, 1931), 22.

12. William Tabbernee, "Dissenting Spiritualities in History," *The Way* 28, no. 2 (1988): 139.

13. Gerald Lewis Bray, *Holiness and the Will of God: Perspectives on the Theology of Tertullian* (Atlanta: John Knox, 1979), 54–63.

14. William Tabbernee, *Montanist Inscriptions and Testimonia: Epigraphic Sources Illustrating the History of Montanism*, Patristic Monograph 16 (Macon, GA: Mercer University Press, 1997), 70–71.

15. Tabbernee, "Dissenting Spiritualities in History," 139.

16. Irenaeus, *Against Heresies*, 1.10.2, in Philip Schaff, *The Apostolic Fathers with Justin Martyr and Irenaeus*, vol. 1 (Buffalo, NY: Christian Literature Company, 1885), 472.

17. J. N. D. Kelly, *Early Christian Doctrines*, 5th ed. (New York: Continuum, 2006), 192.

18. Irenaeus, *Against Heresies*, 3.24.1; Schaff, 662.

19. Irenaeus, *Against Heresies*, 4.18.5; Schaff, 703.

20. Michael Green, *Evangelism in the Early Church* (Grand Rapids, MI: Eerdmans, 1970, 2003), 57. Italics in the original.

21. Timothy George, "The Challenge of Evangelism in the History of the Church," in *Evangelism in the Twenty-First Century: The Critical Issues*, ed. Thom S. Rainer (Wheaton, IL: Harold Shaw, 1989), 10.

22. Tertullian, "The Apology," in *The Ante-Nicene Fathers*, vol. III, eds. Alexander Roberts and James Donaldson (New York: Charles Scribner's Sons, 1903), 45.

CHAPTER 5: CONFLICT WITH THE EMPIRE

1. Allen C. Myers, "Dura-Europos," in *The Eerdmans Bible Dictionary* (Grand Rapids, MI: Eerdmans, 1987), 296.

2. Edward Adams, *The Earliest Christian Meeting Places: Almost Exclusively Houses?*, ed. John M. G. Barclay (London: Bloomsbury, 2013), 89–95.

3. Adams, 83.

4. Adams, 84.

5. Eusebius, *Eusebius' Ecclesiastical History*, 8.1.5, trans. C. F. Cruse (Peabody, MA: Hendrickson, 1998), 279–280.

6. J. N. D. Kelly, *Early Christian Creeds*, 3rd ed. (London: Continuum, 2006), 114.

7. Eusebius, *Eusebius' Ecclesiastical History*, 8.2.4–8.3.4, trans. C. F. Cruse (Peabody, MA: Hendrickson, 1998), 281–282.

CHAPTER 6: THE EMPIRE PERIOD

1. St. Ambrose, "[Letter] Addressed to the Emperor Theodosius after the Massacre at Thessalonica," in *St. Ambrose: Selected Works and Letters*, Select Library of The Nicene and Post-Nicene Fathers of the Christian Church, second series, vol. 10, 51.11, eds. Philip Schaff and Henry Wace, trans. H. De Romestin, E. De Romestin, and H. T. F. Duckworth (New York: Christian Literature Company, 1896), 1031.

2. Mary T. Boatwright et al., *The Romans: From Village to Empire*, 2nd ed. (New York: Oxford University Press, 2012), 426.

3. Remy Lafort, entry for "Lapsi," *The Catholic Encyclopedia*. Public domain. See also Johann Peter Kirsch, "Lapsi," *The Catholic Encyclopedia*, vol. 9 (New York: Robert Appleton, 1910), http://www.newadvent.org/cathen/09001b.htm.

4. St. Cyprian of Carthage, Epistle 70, "To Quintus, Concerning the Baptism of Heretics," trans. Robert Ernest Wallis, *Epistles of Cyprian of Carthage*, New Advent, https://www.newadvent.org/fathers/050670.htm.

5. "Edict of Toleration by Galerius, 311 CE," Center for Online Judaic Studies, accessed September 7, 2022, http://cojs.org/edict_of_toleration _by_galerius-_311_ce.

6. For a good discussion of this period, see Boatwright et al., *The Romans*, 482–486.

7. Athanasius, who was present at the council, put the number of attendees at 318. But most scholars agree that this is a symbolic number taken from Genesis 14:14. They generally believe that the attendance was closer to 250.

8. "The Nicene Creed," in *The Seven Ecumenical Councils*, Select Library of The Nicene and Post-Nicene Fathers of the Christian Church, second series, vol. 14, eds. Henry R. Percival, Philip Schaff, and Henry Wace (New York: Charles Scribner's Sons, 1900), 55.

9. "The First Council of Constantinople, Historical Introduction," in *The Seven Ecumenical Councils*, 437–438.

10. Consider the lengthy and balanced discussion in J. N. D. Kelly, *Early Christian Creeds*, 3rd ed. (London: Continuum, 2006), 305–331.

11. J. N. D. Kelly, *Early Christian Doctrines*, 2nd ed. (New York: Harper & Row, 1960), 339–340. Italics added to show the developments on previous creeds.

12. "The Scriptures Acknowledged by the Roman Church, c. 190," in J. Stevenson, ed., *A New Eusebius: Documents Illustrating the History of the Church to AD 337*, rev. ed. (London: SPCK, 1987), 123. Italics in the original.

13. Stevenson, 123. Italics in the original.

14. It is instructive to compare these standards to Deuteronomy 18:18-22.

15. Stevenson, 124. Italics in the original.

16. Stevenson, 124.

17. Bruce L. Shelley, *Church History in Plain Language* (Waco, TX: Word, 1982), 154.

18. Angelo Di Berardino, Thomas C. Oden, and Joel C. Elowsky, *Encyclopedia of Ancient Christianity*, vol. 3 (Downers Grove, IL: InterVarsity, 2014), 51–52.

19. St. Patrick, "Confession," in Newport J. D. White, *St. Patrick: His Writings and Life*, ed. Eleanor Hull (London: Society for Promoting Christian Knowledge, 1920), 45–46. Italics in the original.

20. Philip Schaff, *History of the Christian Church*, vol. 2, 2nd ed. (New York: Charles Scribner's Sons, 1922), note, 265.

CHAPTER 7: THE EARLY MIDDLE AGES

1. Michael Green, *Evangelism in the Early Church* (Grand Rapids, MI: Eerdmans, 2004), 120–122.

CHAPTER 8: THE HIGH MIDDLE AGES

1. "Waldensians: Medieval 'Evangelicals,'" *Christian History*, issue 22 (1989).

2. A. W. Mitchell, *The Waldenses: Sketches of the Evangelical Christians of the Valleys of Piedmont* (Philadelphia: Presbyterian Board of Publication, 1853), 378.

3. But see the defense of the idea in Alan Cairns, "Waldenses," in *Dictionary of Theological Terms* (Greenville, SC: Ambassador Emerald International, 2002).

4. Mitchell, *The Waldenses*, 28–29.

5. Bruce L. Shelley, *Church History in Plain Language* (Waco, TX: Word, 1982), 231.

CHAPTER 9: THE LATE MIDDLE AGES

1. "Black Death Inspires Zwingli's Plague Hymn," *Christianity Today*, originally published in "Zwingli: Father of the Swiss Reformation,"

Christian History, no. 4 (1984), https://www.christianitytoday.com /history/issues/issue-4/black-death-inspires-zwinglis-plague-hymn.html.

2. Mark Cartwright, "Black Death," *World History Encyclopedia*, March 28, 2020, https://www.worldhistory.org/Black_Death/.

3. See David Allen, "John Wycliffe: Morning Star of the Reformation," Trinitarian Bible Society, 2017, https://www.christianstudylibrary.org /article/john-wycliffe-morning-star-reformation-0.

CHAPTER 10: THE REFORMATION ERA

1. Alister McGrath, *Christianity's Dangerous Idea: The Protestant Revolution: A History from the Sixteenth Century to the Twenty-First* (New York: HarperCollins, 2007), 3.

2. Martin Luther, *The Roots of Reform*, ed. Timothy J. Wengert, vol. 1, The Annotated Luther (Minneapolis, MN: Fortress Press, 2015), 38.

3. Although this is the language from the earliest printing of Luther's remarks, there is some evidence that "Here I stand" was added later on. Martin Luther, *Career of the Reformer*, ed. George Forell, vol. 32, Luther's Works, n.d., 113. n. 8.

4. In at least some cases, the accusations about the Anabaptists appear to have been confused. See note 48 in Robert Kolb, Timothy J. Wengert, and Charles P. Arand, *The Book of Concord: The Confessions of the Evangelical Lutheran Church* (Minneapolis: Fortress, 2000), 40.

5. Roland H. Bainton, *The Reformation of the Sixteenth Century* (Boston: Beacon Press, 1985), 89.

6. Daniel Liechty and Bernard McGinn, eds., *Early Anabaptist Spirituality: Selected Writings* (Mahwah, NJ: Paulist Press, 1994), 3.

7. Erwin W. Lutzer, *Rescuing the Gospel: The Story and Significance of the Reformation* (Grand Rapids, MI: Baker Books, 2016), 158.

8. Lutzer, *Rescuing the Gospel*, 158.

9. John Calvin, *Institutes of the Christian Religion*, vol. 2, ch. 3.6, ed. John T. McNeill, trans. Ford Lewis Battles (Louisville, KY: Westminster John Knox, 2011), 297.

10. Bruce L. Shelley, *Church History in Plain Language* (Waco, TX: Word, 1982), 320.

CHAPTER 11: THE REVIVALISTS

1. Benjamin Franklin, *The Autobiography of Benjamin Franklin* (Bedford, MA: Applewood, 2008), 161.

2. Jonathan ("Rev. President") Edwards, *Sinners in the Hands of an Angry God* (Philadelphia: Presbyterian Board of Publication, 1920), 3, 7.

3. Edwards, *Sinners in the Hands*, 15.

4. C. H. Spurgeon, "Memory—The Handmaid of Hope," October 15,

1865, in *The Metropolitan Tabernacle Pulpit Sermons*, vol. 11 (London: Passmore & Alabaster, 1865), 570.

5. C. H. Spurgeon, *The Sword and Trowel: 1875* (London: Passmore & Alabaster, 1875), 251–252.

6. "Wesleys Oxford: Sharing Stories from the Birthplace of Methodism," The Methodist Church, https://www.wesleysoxford.org.uk/people/holy -club/what-was-the-holy-club.

7. John Wesley, "I Felt My Heart Strangely Warmed," in *The Journal of John Wesley* (Chicago: Moody, 1951), 36.

8. A. J. Broomhall, *Hudson Taylor and China's Open Century, Book Five: Refiner's Fire* (London: Hodder and Stoughton, 1985), 57.

CHAPTER 12: THE CENTURY OF GLOBAL WAR

1. Dietrich Bonhoeffer, *The Cost of Discipleship*, trans. R. H. Fuller (New York: Macmillan, 1963), 99.

2. J. Gresham Machen, *Christianity and Liberalism*, new edition (Grand Rapids, MI: Eerdmans, 2009), 2.

3. "Resolution on Abortion," Southern Baptist Convention annual meeting, June 1, 1971, https://www.sbc.net/resource-library/resolutions/resolution -on-abortion-2.

4. "Resolution on Abortion and Sanctity of Human Life," Southern Baptist Convention annual meeting, June 1, 1974, https://www.sbc.net/resource -library/resolutions/resolution-on-abortion-and-sanctity-of-human-life.

5. "Resolution on Abortion," Southern Baptist Convention annual meeting, June 1, 1976, https://www.sbc.net/resource-library/resolutions/resolution -on-abortion-3.

6. "Resolution on Abortion," Southern Baptist Convention annual meeting, June 1, 1980, https://www.sbc.net/resource-library/resolutions/resolution -on-abortion-6.

7. Billy Graham, "The Whirlwind," sermon at Los Angeles Crusade, September 16, 1949. Audio archive on Billy Graham Evangelistic Association website, https://billygraham.org/audio/the-whirlwind, 38:52–39:16, 39:43–39:52. Transcribed by the author.

8. Robert H. Schuller, "Tough Times Never Last, But Tough People Do," *The Hour of Power*, 1982. Viewed on YouTube, "Robert H. Schuller Sermon on Proverbs 23:7," https://www.youtube.com/watch?v=U _LCsRS38TI, 0:47–1:07, 1:46–2:18. Transcribed by the author.

9. Rick Warren, *The Purpose Driven Church: Growth without Compromising Your Message and Mission* (Grand Rapids, MI: Zondervan, 2007), 80.

10. Warren, *Purpose Driven Church*, 163.

11. World Missionary Conference, *Report of Commission VIII. Co-Operation and the Promotion of Unity. With Supplement: Presentation and Discussion*

of the Report in the Conference on 21st June 1910 (New York: Fleming H. Revell, 1910), 243.

12. Vinson Synan, "Pentecostalism: William Seymour," Christianity Today website, https://www.christianitytoday.com/history/issues/issue-65 /pentecostalism-william-seymour.html. See also Tristan Fenhold, "The African American Roots and Interracial Ideal of the Pentecostal Movement," February 4, 2022, Tristan Fenhold (website), https:// tristanfenholt.com/2022/02/04/the-african-american-roots-and -interracial-ideal-of-the-pentecostal-movement/.

13. Ruth A. Tucker and Walter L. Liefeld, *Daughters of the Church: Women and Ministry from New Testament Times to the Present* (Grand Rapids, MI: Zondervan, 2010).

14. "Maude Jensen, 1904–1998," United Methodist Church General Commission on Archives & History, accessed September 21, 2022, http:// www.gcah.org/site/apps/nlnet/content3.aspx?c=ghKJI0PHIoE&b=3637671 &ct=4506093; "Women Ministers (1955–1966) and Margaret Towner," Presbyterian Outlook, accessed September 21, 2022, https://pres-outlook .org/2006/02/women-ministers-1955-1966-and-margaret-towner/.

15. "My Fight to Become a Woman Priest in Church of England," BBC News, March 12, 2014, https://www.bbc.com/news/av/magazine -26529128. See also Flora Winfield, "A Time of Testing: The Ecumenical Implications of the Ordination of Women as Priests in the Church of England," *Mid-Stream* 33, no. 3 (1994), 299.

CHAPTER 13: THE INFORMATION ERA

1. Justin McCarthy, "Same-Sex Marriage Support Inches Up to New High of 71%," Gallup, June 1, 2022, https://news.gallup.com/poll/393197/same -sex-marriage-support-inches-new-high.aspx.

2. Chris Burgess, "Joyce Lin Memorial," Mission Aviation Fellowship, May 13, 2020, https://hub.maf.org/memorial/joyce-lin-memorial. For more of Joyce Lin's inspiring story, consider obtaining the documentary *To the Ends of the Earth* from https://endsoftheearthmovie.com.

About the Author

JUSTIN GATLIN has served as senior pastor of Alvin Missionary Baptist Church since January 2018. He is part of the faculty of Texas Baptist Institute and Seminary in Henderson, Texas, and oversees the school's extension learning center in Alvin, Texas. He has written VBS curriculum for Bogard Press and is the author of *Journey through the Old Testament*. He lives in Alvin with his wife, Colleen, and their three children: Anastasia, Samuel, and Josiah.